NOT TO BE TAKEN AWAY

Playground Design

London Borough of Enfield	
91200000256472	
ASKEWS & HOLT	22-Jun-2012
711.558	£45.00

Playground Design

Michelle Galindo

BRAUN

CONTENTS

6 Preface

Fantasy

12 **Dragon Playground**
pro garten landschaftsarchitektur

16 **The Cargoship in Höganäs**
Monstrum

20 **Pirate Bay**
Zimmer.Obst playground design

24 **The Other Star - Playground Dossestraße**
birke zimmermann Landschaftsarchitekten

28 **Brumleby**
Monstrum

32 **Anansi**
Mulders vandenBerk Architecten

36 **The Bermuda Triangle**
Monstrum

40 **"The Dream" Playground**
pro garten landschaftsarchitektur

44 **The Giant Spider and the Mushrooms**
Monstrum

48 **Play Ship Playground**
Zimmer.Obst playground design

52 **Tower of Copenhagen Playground**
Monstrum

56 **Playground in Belleville Park**
BASE

60 **The Dragon's Castle**
Zimmer.Obst playground design

64 **Dragon Land**
E.F.E.U. Riederer und Münch

68 **Rasmus Klump**
Monstrum

72 **Warnitzer Arches**
Zimmer.Obst playground design

Nature

78 **Crater Lake**
24° Studio

82 **Vondelpark Canopy Walk**
Carve

86 **Dry Cleaning II: "Fall into the Moon"**
AMMA architecture de paysage

90 **Water Playground in Hemer**
Geskes & Hack design studio

94 **Tapachtal Playground**
Kunder³ Landschaftarchitektur

96 **Sculptural Playground**
ANNABAU Architektur und Landschaft

100 **Darling Quarter**
Aspect Studios

104 **Rooke Reserve**
CPG Australia

108 **Kilburn Grange Park Play Center and Park**
Erect Architecture

112 **Atoll Playground**
geske.hack landscape architects

116 **Playgrounds of the National Garden Show Norderstedt**
plancontext landschaftsarchitektur

120 **Dymaxion Sleep**
Jane Hutton & Adrian Blackwell

124 **Heights Park Killesberg**
Rainer Schmidt Landschaftsarchitekten

126 **Vondelpark Towers**
Carve

130 **Stud Park Playground**
Jeavons Landscape Architects

134 **Stone's Throw Playground**
LAND-I archicolture

136 **Monte Laa Central Park**
Martha Schwartz Partners

140 **Atlantis Playground**
plancontext landschaftsarchitektur

144 **BUGA**
Rainer Schmidt Landschaftsarchitekten

148 **Water Playground**
RS+

152 **Garden City Play Environment**
Space2place

156 Safe Zone
Stoss Landscape Urbanism

158 "Im Gefilde" Playground
ver.de Landschaftsarchitektur

162 Central Park
Rainer Schmidt Landschaftsarchitekten

Sports
---

166 Potgieterstraat
Carve

170 Wikado Playground
2012 Architecten

174 Playground Fence
Atelier Remy & Veenhuizen

176 Van Campenvaart
Carve

180 Park des Prés de Lyon,
La Chapelle Saint-Luc
BASE

184 Urban Dock LaLaport Toyosu
EARTHSCAPE

188 Public Playground Rotterdam
Bekkering Adams Architecten

192 Bijlmerpark
Carve in collaboration with Marie-Laure Hoedemakers

196 Lazona Kawasaki Plaza
EARTHSCAPE

200 KuKuk Playground
KuKuk

204 St Mary's Churchyard
Martha Schwartz Partners

208 Van Beuningenplein
Carve

212 Merida Factory Youth Movement
selgascano

216 Pole Dance
SO-IL

220 Playground Building
Van Rooijen Nourbakhsh Architecten

224 Wall-Holla
Carve

228 RUS Lima, Public Amusement Autopark
Basurama

230 Umbraculum and Children's Games Garden
Navadijos Tarsoly Arquitectos

234 Architects' Index

239 Photo Credits

240 Imprint

PREFACE

Where did the conception of playgrounds begin?
by Michelle Galindo

The first playgrounds began with promoting health and recreation, issuing playground standards, continuing with interactive products going on to the market and with the need of putting children away from the streets rising. After analyzing the free, uninhibited play and exploration of children, unusual play structures based upon new pedagogical ideas on children's development were developed. Moreover, the safety regulations and the use of safer materials increased. The stimulation of creativity and imagination and increasing physical activity is the driving force of playground design today.

Images of swings are present in art as early as the 5th century B.C.; Greek vase painters captured life's more playful moments, including women and children playing on a swing. And while such evidence suggests that swings are an ancient notion, the modern concept of playground equipment, as we know it today began in the United States at the turn of the 20th century, amidst cultural and economic reforms.

In the late 19th century, when child labor laws successfully increased the minimum working age, newly idle children had no safe place to play in urban areas. A movement backed by women and educators in many private associations set aside space and created playground equipment. In 1920, the first playground standards were issued and The National Recreation Association began publishing recommendations for school playground equipment. Soon after that Sebastian Hinton patented the "Jungle Gym", three-dimensional playground equipment on which children could climb as a form of exercise and play. Playgrounds grew rapidly across the United States in 1930, during the Great Depression and were funded by the Federal Government. In 1940 World War II put a damper on the manufacture of new playground equipment and many fell into disrepair.

In 1943, the first "adventure playground" was designed by C. Th. Sørensen, a Danish landscape architect. Here, children could create and shape, dream and imagine a reality. The movement of adventure playgrounds spread throughout Europe. In Switzerland, the first two playgrounds opened in 1955, and in Germany in 1967. These recreational facilities featured rope ladders, pyramids, and many other types of climbing apparatus, predominantly made from steel. They were often designed by architects and were beautiful urban spaces.

New safety regulations in the 1980s included recommendations for removing had equipment (metal bars) by substituting soft materials such as wood and plastic. The change to wooden swing sets accelerated through the 1990s, and injuries from the playground equipment lessened. In the 1990s, further guidelines brought finely tuned sensitivity to safety issues in playgrounds' design. At the beginning of the 21st century, wooden playground equipment continued to accelerate. Today the concern with children's health has given rise to an increased interest in outdoor play, shifting design into more provocative and bold structures.

Despite significant changes over more than a century in the equipment and appearance of playgrounds, as their designs have evolved, one thing has remained constant – the essential role that the playgrounds play in the vitality of urban neighborhoods, and in particular the physical development and socialization of children. Not only is a playground a place where a child may fly down a slide, soar on a swing, scale heights on a play structure, or be cooled by a spray shower, but it is also a critical part of a child's emotional education, where he or she discovers perhaps for the first time the challenges of the world outside the home.

A lack of resources, limited budgets and our society's obsession over minimizing risk are the main cause for the standardized design of most playgrounds. While these playgrounds may be fun initially, they rarely sustain a child's interest on repeated visits. Today, technological advancements have allowed an ever-increasing body of talented architects, landscape architects and artists, in collaboration with manufacturers, that combine play, adventure, fantasy and safety into their designs, ultimately creating a spatial arena for children to support their boundless imagina-

PREFACE

tions at a manageable scale. The many practitioners showcased within these pages are striving to make playground design the next revolution, placing children at the center of their design process as a simple extension of their vision to create play environments that are rich in creativity, arts and inspiration to reach ecological health.

Their designs act "outside the box", using imagination as the main design element, exploring material properties and keeping in mind that play is an important role in the development of children; their ideas are born from a visual story that creates a space where fantasy thrives, open up possibilities for free, uninhibited play and exploration, and meet the needs of today's youth. They apply a wide-ranging selection of imaginative solutions in playground design, programs which combine the needs of creating an entertaining, exciting and stimulating environment on the one hand and, on the other, providing an aesthetically pleasing public space, while also ensuring that the necessary safety requirements are met. Included are the design components (surface materials, different types of swings and slides, climbing equipment) as well as the functional considerations (different types of activities for different age groups).

Playground Design exemplifies the best of high quality playgrounds, showcasing from fantasy, nature-based and sports playgrounds with different designed themes such as, dragons, ships, animals, towers, pirates, trees and an organically shaped structure, simulating a plastic "cloud", among many others.

In the fantasy playgrounds there is a story plot where children become the actors and adopt roles which they are able to fulfill with their imagination. The designers provide the set, in which the children should act upon. The colorful playgrounds of Monstrum are based on storytelling, they create a visual story to teach and entertain the children. For instance, *The Tower Playground* in Copenhagen's Fælledparken in Denmark invites children into a fantasyland where they will feel like giants. The playground is comprised of five towers modeled after real Copenhagen towers. The towers in the playground are connected by slides and bridges, allowing the children to climb and play among the rooftops of a miniature city. The replica towers give them a close up look at some of the city's most important architecture.

No matter how poor, colorless and toyless their environment is, children always find a way to play. They play with stones, twigs, grass and water. They think up ways of turning mundane items into creations. The designers' inspiration for the nature-based playgrounds featured in this book, was born from this basic way of playing. Their projects respond to their surrounding context, develop awareness for natural systems and provide a rich diversity of play and learning experiences. While the designers include elements suitable for specific age groups, the malleable elements of sand and water that link all these elements act as a social catalyst. Children are invited to embark in an adventure high above the trees and across bridges or to soak themselves in water basins. The *Water Playground* in Tychy, Poland by RS+ matches its surrounding landscape and contour of the basin, while at the same time colorful aquatic toys allow functional, constructive and dramatic play, giving the children a chance to improve their motor skills and develop their social skills. These play environments were designed to allow children to experience risks and test their boundaries without exposure to hazard. The result is a design that provides open-ended play experiences that encourage imagination and creative play while meeting the emotional, cognitive and physical needs of children.

To attract the youth, a sturdier and bigger arena with bold design welcomes an older generation into an open and safe field, stimulating physical skills and abilities beyond the excessively abundant media entertainment available. Selgascano's curvaceous skate park, *Mérida Factory Youth Movement* in Mérida, Spain provides the youth with a place to skateboard, dance hip-hop, climb rocks and create graffiti. This playground melts arts, sports and inspiration in a colorful, open and inviting plastic "cloud" structure. Sports playgrounds teach children about the importance of key values and to deal with competition. These learning aspects highlight the impact of physical education and sport on a child's social and moral development. This pedagogic theory is the basic layer of the programmatic design idea.

Focusing on the immersion of a world of play and exploration, this volume presents 58 outstanding, recent interpretations of "meaning" in playground design worldwide, each meeting the requirements that contribute to ideal spaces for children, combined with innovative design practices. As society and technology changes, playground design will continue to develop and weak up the curiosity and creativity in children, as well as the inner child in its creators.

FANTASY

FANTASY

pro garten
landschaftsarchitektur

↑ | **The castle**

Dragon Playground
Berlin

The thematic playground Dragon Playground was conceived for children aged six years and younger. It is situated in a building gap with the castle hill rising at the rear wall of the plot. The dragon lurking in the sand is conquered from the castle. The dragon is a sequence of different climbing and balancing equipment. Its wings consist of a bird's nest swing and a hammock. A dragon nest seesaw featuring dragon's eggs complements the equipment. A paved path surrounding the sand area can be used for moving around the playground and for toys on wheels. The playground can be observed from a promenade along the street planted with cherry plums. An unpaved path leads through a jungle of hazelnut bushes, complementing the paths.

PROJECT FACTS **Address:** Ebersstraße 85/86, 10827 Berlin, Germany. **Client:** district office of Tempelhof-Schöneberg in Berlin, Department of Environment and Nature. **Play design:** ZimmerObst Spielraumgestaltung. **Completion:** 2008. **Materials:** black locust, oak (playground equipment), concrete pavement, sand, bark mulch (flooring) and limestone blocks. **Theme:** the dragon and the castle.

↑ | The dragon
↓ | Small dragon

↓ | Dragon's nest, rocker and swing

FANTASY   PRO GARTEN LANDSCHAFTSARCHITEKTUR

DRAGON PLAYGROUND

↖↑ | View from the castle to the dragon
←← | Sketch
← | Dragon castle and tunnel

FANTASY | Monstrum

↑ | Light house

The Cargoship in Höganäs
Höganäs Marina

A cargo shipwreck was constructed for Höganäs Municipality in Sweden as a part of a larger renovation project of the surrounding park area. A huge cargo ship has sunken and is now on the ocean floor next to the lighthouse between cargo crates and fish. Everything is very chaotic. The children move along a dangerous route between loose boxes and driftwood. Inside the hull the kids explore dangerous adventures and balance on debris only to finally flee to safety at the lighthouse, away from the dangers of the ocean.

PROJECT FACTS **Address:** Höganäs Marina, Sweden. **Client:** Höganäs municipality, Sweden. **Completion:** 2008. **Materials:** wood, metal and sand. **Theme:** maritime.

↑ | Cargoship front detail
↓ | Cargoship with a slide, sinking in the sand

FANTASY   MONSTRUM

THE CARGOSHIP IN HÖGANÄS

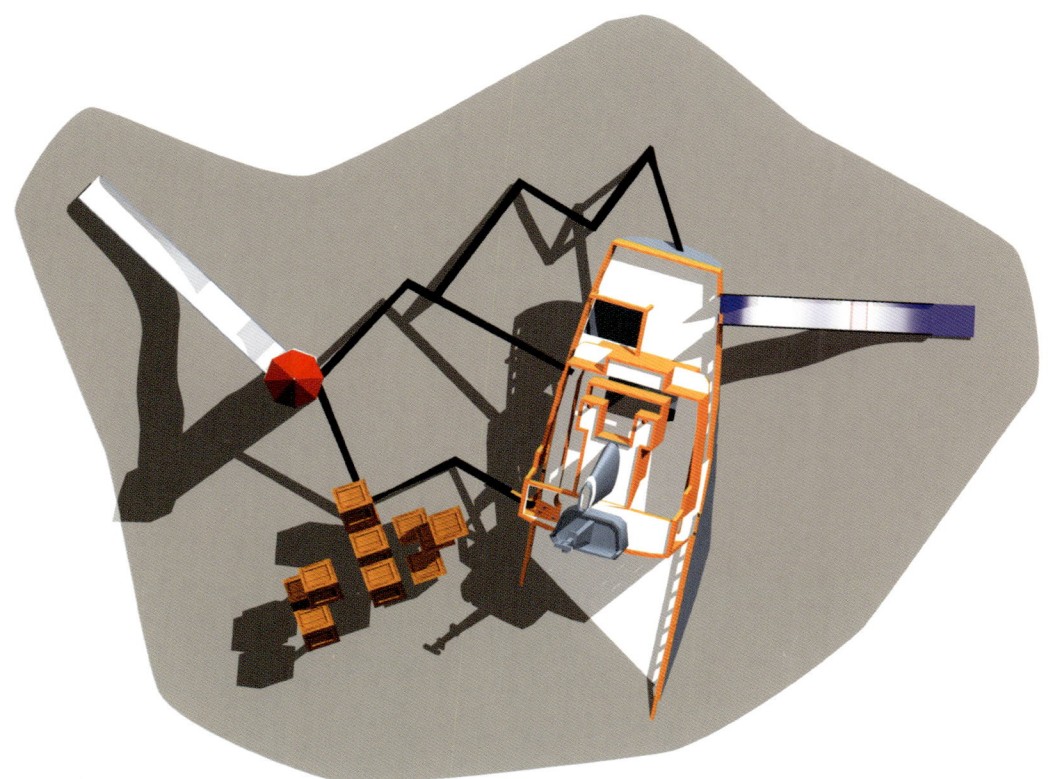

↖↖ | Cargoship boxes
←← | General view
↑ | Cargo boxes used to move around playground
← | Top view

FANTASY | Zimmer.Obst playground design

↑ | **Pirate Bay towers connected with hammocks, rope bridges and slides**

Pirate Bay
Stadtallendorf

The 1,230 square meter area was divided into three adjacent play areas with a "pirate" theme. The fishing village, for children aged 3-6 years, offers playhouses with fishing equipment, as well as crates, bow nets, and fishing nets. An abstract shipwreck with a mast and a crow's nest is at the heart of the area as a combining element. The pirate bay is a fortress-like structure for children aged 6 years and above. All three areas feature a variety of play functions of different difficulty levels, allowing all age groups to enjoy playing. The entire playground contains play houses, sand play areas, climbing walls, hammocks, swings, suspended bridges, slides, and much more. Traces and remnants of "cannonballs" in the walls promise exciting stories of gold and treasure and the hunt for both.

PROJECT FACTS   **Address:** Waldstraße, 35260 Stadtallendorf, Germany. **Client:** Stadtallendorf City Council. **Landscapes architects:** Latz Riehl Partner Landschaftsarchitekten. **Planning design:** Carsten Obst. **Completion:** 2010. **Materials:** wood, ropes, metal and sand. **Theme:** pirates.

↑ | Climbing wall with holding grips and metal tubes for sliding
↓ | Playhouses and barrels

FANTASY ZIMMER.OBST PLAYGROUND DESIGN

↑ | Pirate bay
← | Pirate nest
↗ | Bird's-eye view
→ | Fishing village

PIRATE BAY

FANTASY | birke · zimmermann landschaftsarchitekten

↑ | General view

The Other Star Playground Dossestraße
Berlin

Located in a former gap in the middle of the dense urban landscape of Berlin, the playground contains artificial shapes and colors that were deliberately chosen to be anchored in the mental topography of residents. Designed especially for younger children, the new play area features stars and planets as colored patches and orange equipment as the predominant color. Made of mastic asphalt and painted with star ornaments, a "Milky way" winds around an amorphous play area, which contains, in addition to classical equipment, two colored play hills made of smoothed sprayed concrete with an integrated slide and a trampoline.

PROJECT FACTS   **Address:** Dossestraße 19, 10247 Berlin, Germany. **Client:** district of Friedrichshain / Kreuzberg Office for the Environment and Nature in Cooperation with BSM – Rehabilitation instruct the State of Berlin. **Completion:** 2011. **Materials:** asphalt, concrete, sand, wood, metal, rubber and soil applications. **Theme:** playing field with artificial planets, stars and aliens.

↑ | **Sliding and climbing hills**
↓ | **Aliens for riding**

FANTASY BIRKE · ZIMMERMANN LANDSCHAFTSARCHITEKTEN

← | Rod forest in snow
↓ | Trampoline

THE OTHER STAR – PLAYGROUND DOSSESTRASSE

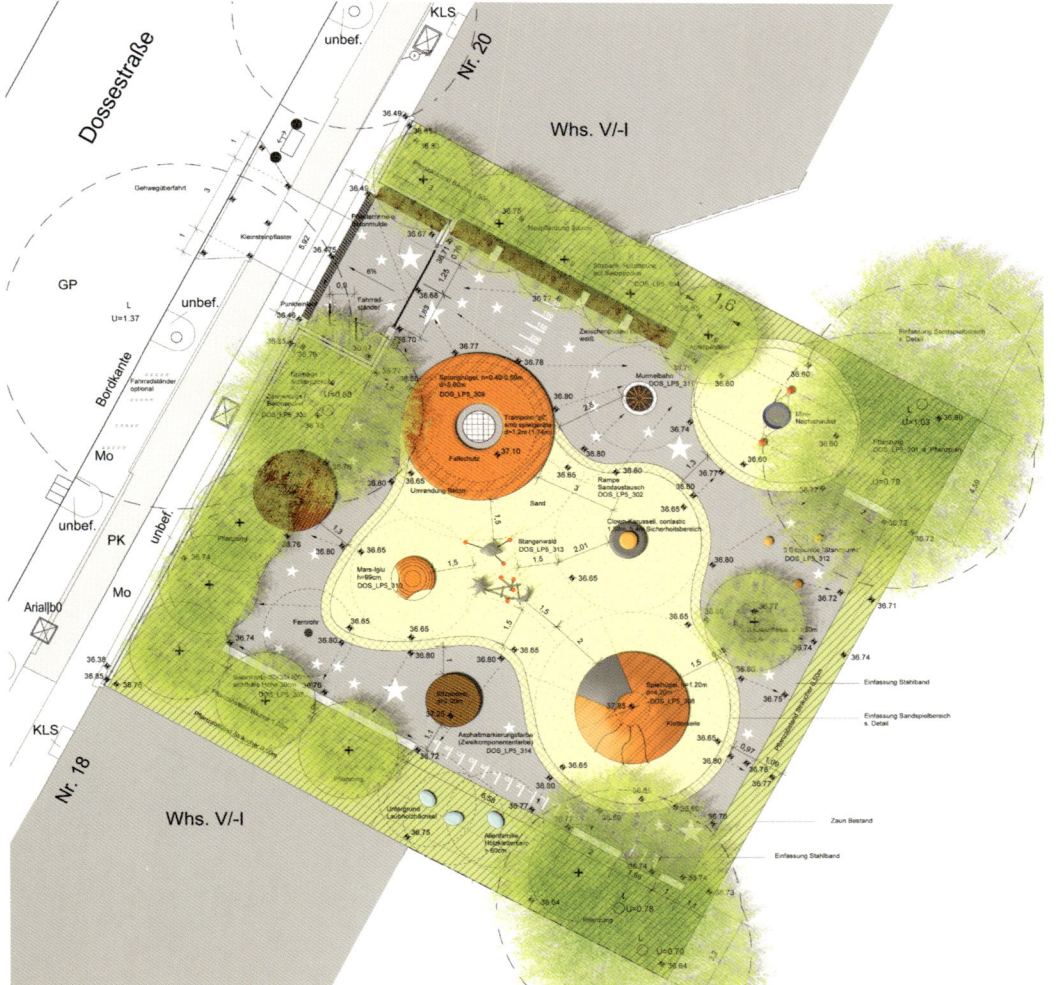

↑ | Bench and ground with painted stars
← | Site plan

FANTASY | Monstrum

↑ | General view

Brumleby
Copenhagen

Brumleby is one of Copenhagen's architectonic culture gems. In 1997, Brumleby was awarded the Europa Nostras prize for its preservation and renovation. The objective of the playground was to add an element to Brumleby that would reflect the nature of the neighborhood as well as turn everything topsy-turvy. Back in those days in the 1800s, when Brumleby was located in the countryside, it had a dairy and a slaughterhouse. The idea of the playground was to recreate a piece of the old Brumleby. The Brumleby playground had to be a pretty sight for adults, fun to play in for the little ones and, preferably, remind us of the fantastic history of Brumleby.

PROJECT FACTS **Address:** Brumleby, Vester Voldgade 17, Copenhagen, Denmark. **Client:** Brumleby General Cooperative Housing Association. **Completion:** 2008. **Materials:** artificial turf, wood and rope. **Theme:** Brumleby's history.

↑ | Suspended bridge connecting housing towers
↓ | Slanted entrance to housing tower

↓ | Window detail

FANTASY　　　　　　　MONSTRUM

← | Curved housing tower
↓ | Front view to bent housing towers

BRUMLEBY

↑ | Entrance to bent housing tower
← | Housing tower with slide

FANTASY | Mulders vandenBerk Architecten

↑ | Interior with a black chalk board surface

Anansi
Utrecht

Mulders vandenBerk Architecten of Amsterdam completed a playground building in a park in Utrecht, the Netherlands, with a Corian façade engraved with images of fairytales from around the world. The idea of the building is to excite and stimulate curiosity and creativity of children. The pavilion splits the playground in two. One side is used by teenagers, the other by young children. The interior is divided into three separate playrooms featuring bright colors, simple furniture, and interactive elements. The design invites children to play, to discover and invent games. The exterior of the building is the opposite of the "active" playground with its many climbing frames and slides, turning the building into a calm oasis in the playground area.

PROJECT FACTS   **Address:** Peltlaan 130, 3527 EC Utrecht, The Netherlands. **Client:** municipality of Utrecht, department D.M.O. **Graphic design façade:** DesignArbeid. **Completion:** 2009. **Materials:** corian (façade). **Theme:** fairytales engraved on façade.

↑ | Exterior play area
↓ | Interior, children painting on chalk board surface

↓ | Corian façade with engraved fairytale images

FANTASY MULDERS VANDENBERK ARCHITECTEN

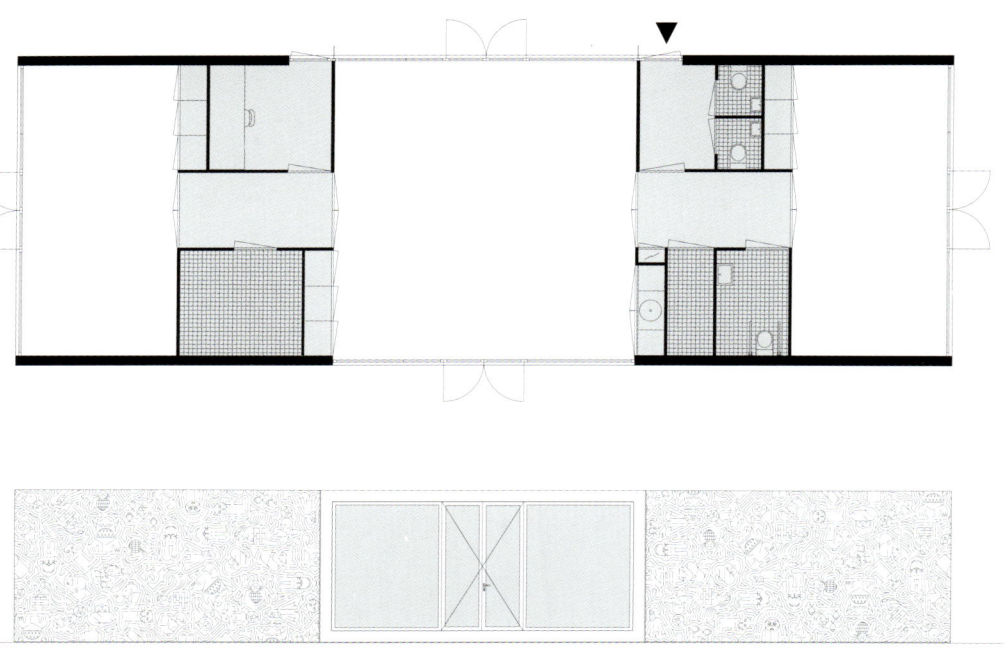

↑ | **Detail of corian façade**
← | **Floor plan**

↑ | Colorful interior with glass wall
← | Interactive colorful interior

FANTASY | Monstrum

↑ | Wrecked plane piece for entering and climbing

The Bermuda Triangle
Copenhagen

MONSTRUM was assigned to upgrade the playground and add new challenges, especially for older children. The playground was designed in cooperation with GHB Landscape Architects for the City of Copenhagen. The playground tells the story of a pilot who has been on a long expedition across the Bermuda Triangle, when he loses control of his plane and drops towards the sea. There are various wrecks of planes and ships, while the survivors of a shipping accident have managed to save themselves on board the lifeboat as a playful emerges and saves them. At the same time, a crew of whale catchers wants to harpoon the whale. The playground consists of a wrecked plane in two parts, the rear end of a galleon, a slide, swings, a whale, a rescue ship, a sandbox and many balancing challenges.

PROJECT FACTS **Address:** Nørrebro Park, Hørsholmsgade 32, 2200 Copenhagen, Denmark. **Client:** Copenhagen municipality. **Landscape architects:** GHB Landscape Architects. **Completion:** 2008. **Materials:** wood. **Theme:** the Bermuda Triangle.

↑ | Front view of wrecked plane
↓ | Wrecked plane in two parts

FANTASY   MONSTRUM

← | Side view of galleon surface used for climbing
↓ | The rear end of a galleon serves as support for the slide
→ | Life boat
↘ | Plan view

THE BERMUDA TRIANGLE

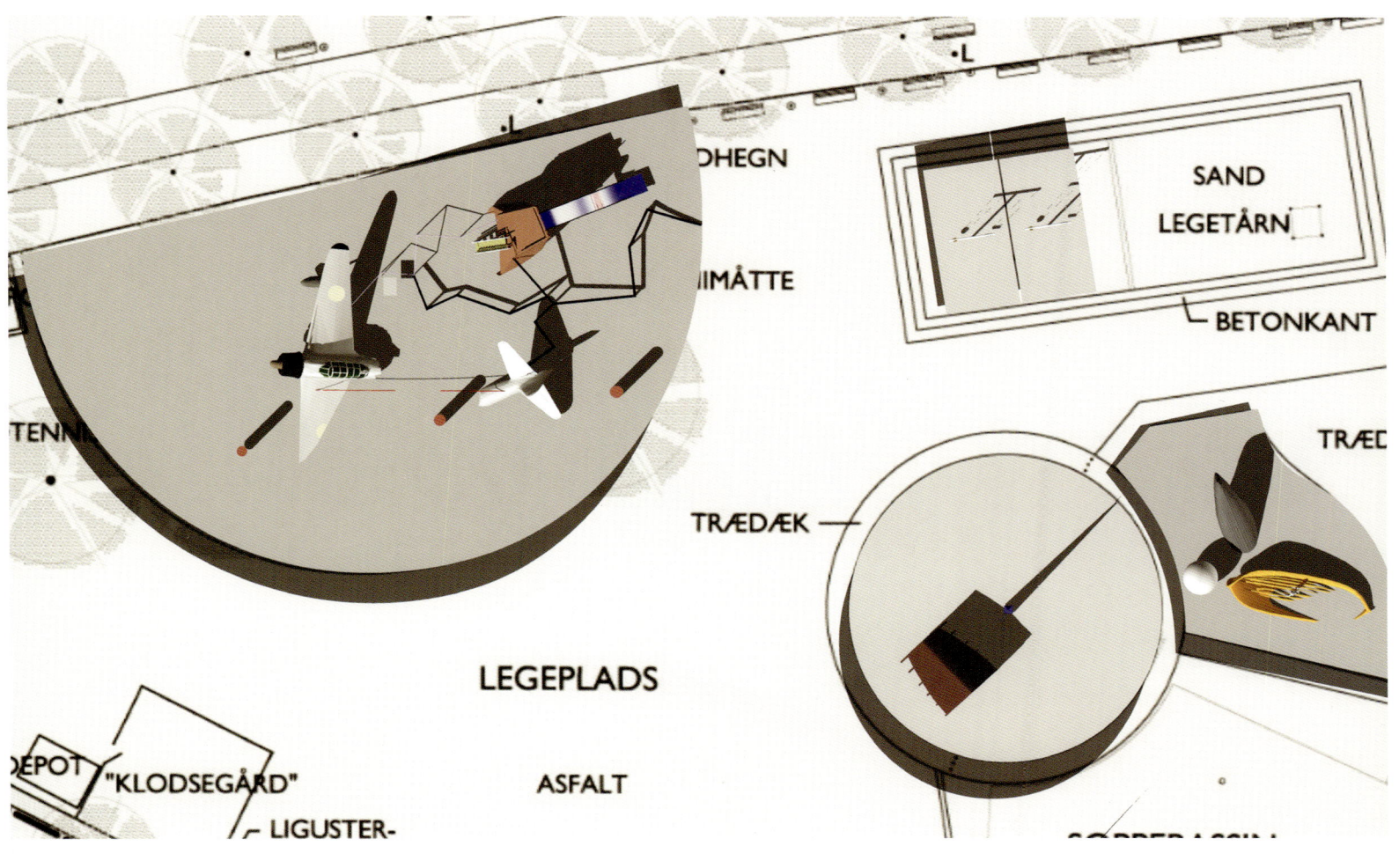

SAND
LEGETÅRN
BETONKANT
TRÆDÆK
TRÆD
LEGEPLADS
ASFALT
DEPOT "KLODSEGÅRD"
LIGUSTER-

FANTASY

pro garten
landschaftsarchitektur

↑ | **Climbing route**

"The Dream" Playground
Berlin

The thematic playground "The Dream" was designed for youths as well as younger children. The design reflects the future dreams of the youths and children. The playground offers motor activity equipment as well as places for relaxation. "Dream bubbles" inserted into a paved area offer play facilities such as trampolines, table tennis, or sand pits, along with seating opportunities. A climbing range, the "dream catcher strip" with nets, net bridges, tunnels and ropes encloses the playground. The covered "Dream catcher cottage" serves as a meeting point for youths. Trees, complemented by large hedges and robust shrubs, constitute the greenery.

PROJECT FACTS **Address:** Hans-Otto-Straße 8–10 / Hufelandstraße, 10407 Berlin, Germany. **Client:** Pankow district of Berlin, Department of Environment and Nature. **Wood design:** Tilman Stachat. **Completion:** 2010. **Materials:** wood, steel, rope (playground equipment), concrete paving, wood chips, sand, EPDM rubber (flooring). **Theme:** dreams.

↑ | **Climbing route "dreamcatcher band"**
↓ | **View to bird's nest in sand area**

FANTASY PRO GARTEN LANDSCHAFTSARCHITEKTUR

"THE DREAM" PLAYGROUND

←← | General view
↙↙ | Sketch
← | Dreamcatcher tower
↓ | Bird's nest to climb and dream

FANTASY | Monstrum

↑ | Net in between spider's legs for climbing

The Giant Spider and the Mushroom
Hilleroed

Copenhagen Housing Association collaborated with local children and Henrik Jørgensen Landscape architect in the design of an adventurous playground featuring a giant spider on its way across the forest floor. With a leg span of 6.5 x 10.5 meters, and a height of 4.8 meters, children can climb into the body of the spider like a tree house. The interior of the spider is diffused in warm LED light at night. The spider has a web between its legs that allows climbing from leg to leg and steel bars for the arms. Next to the spider are three big mushrooms, the largest of which is equipped with a slide. Behind the spider there are large blades of grass in two shades of green to give the impression of movement. The ropes between the blades also offer exciting climbing possibilities.

PROJECT FACTS **Address:** Hilleroed, Denmark. **Client:** Copenhagen, Housing Association, Hilleroed Denmark. **Other creatives:** Walter Blackwell / Carole Courtois & Dany Fillion. **Completion:** 2011. **Materials:** wood, ropes, metal and EPDM rubber. **Theme:** tales from the nature.

↑ | Front view of giant spider
↓ | Spider's interior features LED lighting

↓ | Spider's legs and giant mushroom

FANTASY   MONSTRUM

THE GIANT SPIDER AND THE MUSHROOM

47

←← | Giant mushroom features a slide
↑ | Large grass blades for climbing
← | Top view

FANTASY | Zimmer.Obst playground design

↑ | Ship split in half

Play Ship Playground
Herford

The construction project constitutes one of Herford's most important inner city squares. A play ship was chosen as the key component of the new design. Water is the major element in the plan that involves a generously proportioned water play area with terraces and tools for damming up and controlling the water flow of the large 0ater pool. The ship consists of two parts that were pre-constructed and assembled on site. It had to be planned precisely as it was connected to an existing stainless steel pool. It also includes play and climbing equipment such as a suspended bridge and an individually placed mast with a crow's nest, as well as a treasure chest and slide. Oak wood was chosen as the material for the basic structure while the curved planks of the bow and stern are made of larch wood.

PROJECT FACTS

Address: Linnenbauerplatz, 32052 Herford, Germany. **Client:** City Council Herford. **Landscape architects:** Atelier Dreiseitl. **Design:** Carsten Obst. **Completion:** 2008. **Materials:** oak and larch wood and rubber. **Theme:** play ship.

↑ | Ship interior
↓ | Treasure box inside ship

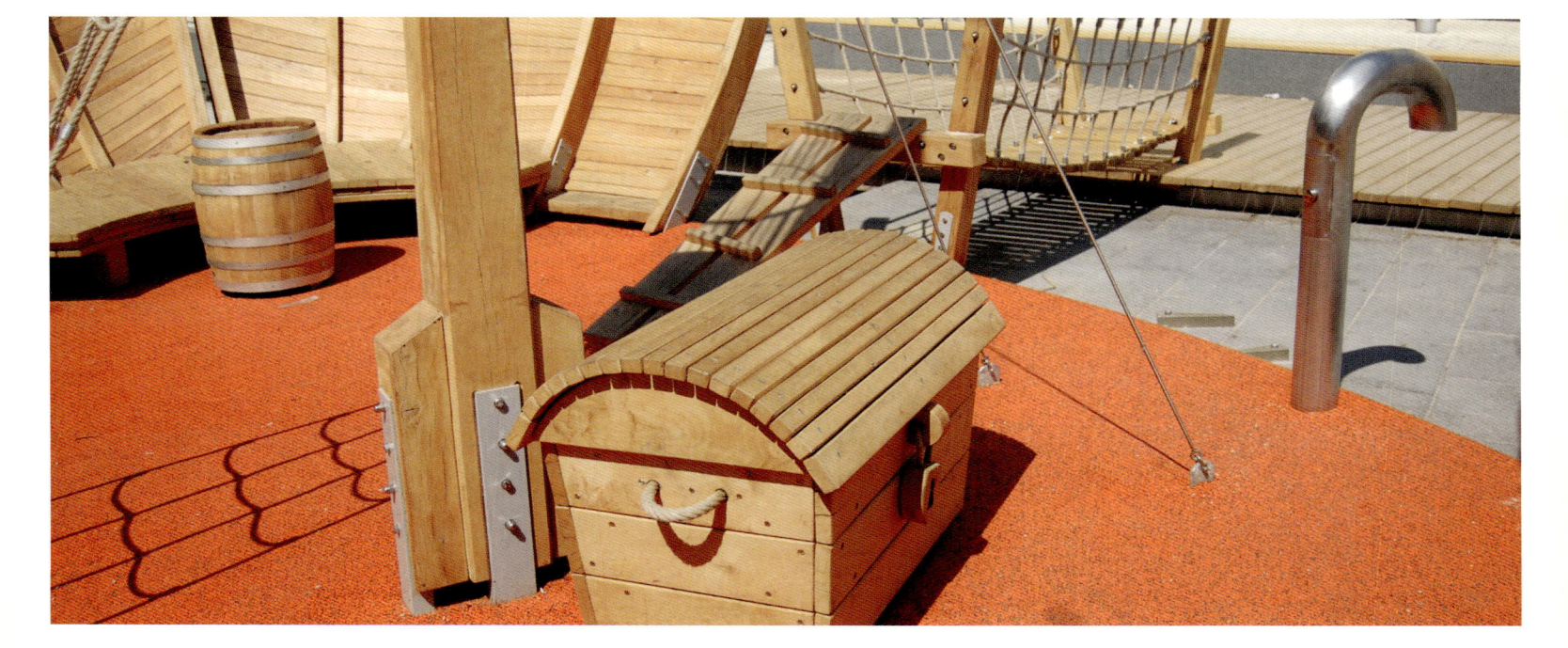

FANTASY ZIMMER.OBST PLAYGROUND DESIGN

↑ | Side view
← | Small slide

PLAY SHIP PLAYGROUND

← | Small window leads to slide
↓ | General view

FANTASY | Monstrum

↖↖ | **Bridge connecting the towers**
↖ | **View to Round Tower**
↑ | **Children climb up to "Our Saviour's Church"**

Tower of Copenhagen Playground
Copenhagen

If a child wants to feel big, it should go to "Fælledparken" and visit the playground towers, with their opportunities for active play and technological interaction. Children can play with electronic tags over the rooftops, solve a rebus in the Round Tower, or hold speeches from the Town Hall Tower. The playground teaches historical facts about Copenhagen's towers, which are part of a motor challenging playground, using technology for high physical activity. The Round Tower features an interior ramp that winds around the tower to the planetarium. Children can then slide down or take rope bridges to the Town Hall Tower, or climb the silhouette to Our Savior's Church to play on the church bells. All towers are made of larch planks and birch plywood with waterproof paint.

PROJECT FACTS **Address:** Fælledparken Copenhagen, Denmark. **Client:** City of Copenhagen. **Collaborating architects:** GHB architects. **Completion:** 2011. **Materials:** larch planks and birch wood, ropes and sand. **Theme:** city towers.

↑ | Towers equipped with slides
↓ | Interior of "City Hall Tower"

↓ | Children slide down the Round Tower slide

FANTASY · MONSTRUM

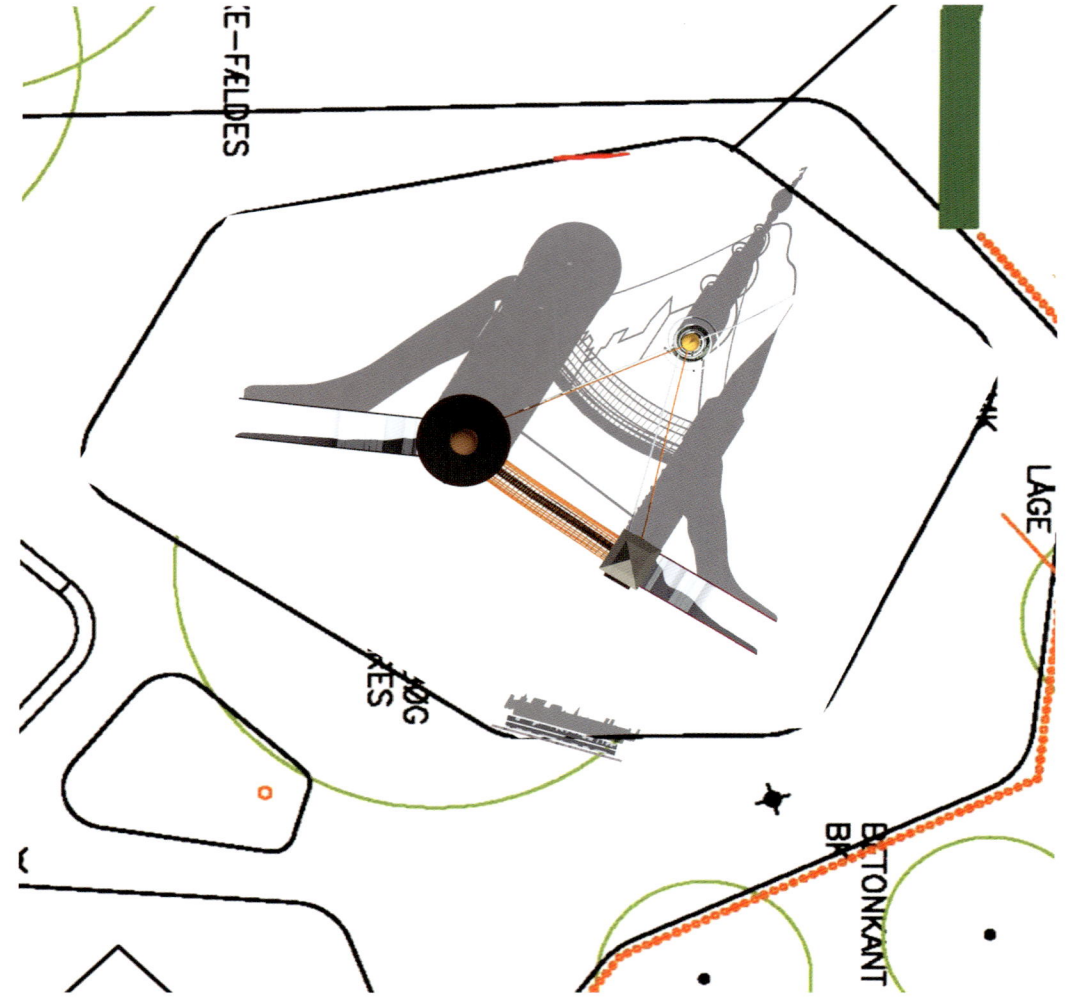

↑ | Children climb up and slide across the towers
← | Top view
↗ | "Stock Exchange" play tower
→ | The "Marble Church" play structure

TOWER OF COPENHAGEN PLAYGROUND

FANTASY | BASE

↑ | **Aerial view**

Playground in Belleville Park
Paris

Located on a high-pitched slope, the playground offers a climbing course with different inclinations for different skill levels and age groups. The inspiration for the design came from the playhouse, which can be designed in several versions: tree dwelling, troglodyte, forest, etc. There is also an urban, interior and minimal version, which is built from scratch with a mattress in the bedroom, a chair, broom sticks and stretched bath towels. It can be turned into a boat, a suspended or a medieval castle, it suits all interpretations and abstractions: it is intelligent. At the same time, the space contains various items offering flexible play possibilities: a mountain landscape, building site, flying carpet, machicolation, medieval fortifications, pirate ship rails, etc.

PROJECT FACTS **Address:** 47 rue des Couronnes, 75020 Paris, France. **Client:** City of Paris, Direction des Parcs, Jardins et Espaces Verts. **Engineer:** Terrasol. **Design consultant:** Luc Mas. **Completion:** 2008. **Materials:** timber pylons, ropes and metal. **Theme:** free-flowing and powerful.

↑ | Pirate ship rails for climbing and sliding
↓ | Inclined surface with hiking holds

↓ | Detail of ropes used for climbing

FANTASY BASE

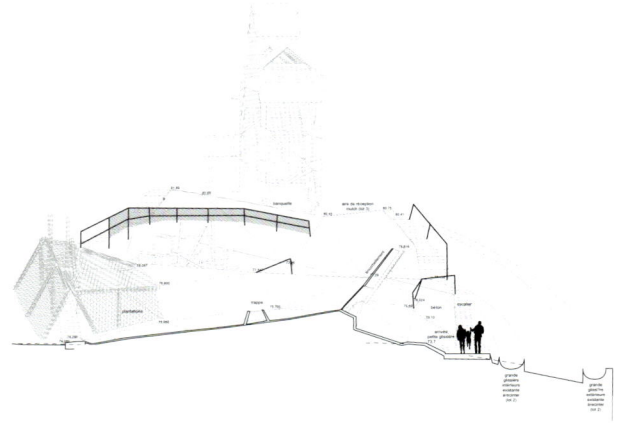

↑ | Top view of stairs and hiking inclined surface
← | Sections
→ | Interior of abstract boat with city views

PLAYGROUND IN BELLEVILLE PARK

FANTASY | Zimmer.Obst playground design

↑ | General view

The Dragon's Castle
Hofstade

The adventure playground is based on the theme "Middle Ages". It contains several play areas, including the Dragon's Castle – a jungle gym made of black locust wood offering challenging climbing opportunities for children aged 6 to 12 years. A tubular slide is situated in the inner castle ward starting at a height of 2 meters. The stainless steel tube passes through the ground underneath the "old water mill" building to emerge on the slope in front of the castle in the shape of a small "hunting lodge". The castle is surrounded by a climbing wall made of concrete elements with recessed climbing grips. Other elements include a blacksmith's shop, a balancing stretch, and a tavern. All include playground equipment in various unusual shapes, offering a wealth of discoveries and adventures.

PROJECT FACTS **Location:** Hofstade, Belgium. **Client:** City of Hofstade Bloso. **Planning:** Krambamboul. **Design:** Frank Zimmer. **Completion:** 2009. **Materials:** concrete (wall), wood, rope and metal. **Theme:** Middle Ages fairy tale.

↑ | **Rope ladder and net for climbing**
↓ | **Water wheel leads to the old forge, then to the tavern**

↑ | **Children climb up to tower and slide down a metal pole**

FANTASY   ZIMMER.OBST PLAYGROUND DESIGN

THE DRAGON'S CASTLE

↖↖ | Bridge leads to the Medieval castle
←← | Bridge leads to Dragon's Castle
↑ | Clock tower with slide
← | Dragon illustration

FANTASY | E.F.E.U. Riederer und Münch

↑ | **Dragon head watches over the playground**

Dragon Land
Berlin

A huge, colorful dragonhead watches over the playground "Dragon Land"; the children climb over a net and a boardwalk to the dragon's head to discover the slides. As part of an intensive participatory process, the 1,470 square meter large playground area was designed for children between 6-10 years old. A sand play area for younger children is ideal for building sandcastles, while slightly older children can prove a double swing und climb trees. The two large sand play areas have been complemented by an "enchanted forest", spring rockers and strains of a "dragon" in which small children like to hide. A seating steps system of sandstone slabs provide relaxation for parents while their children explore the "Dragon Land". Similarly, The playground is complemented by a centrally located water feature area.

PROJECT FACTS **Address:** Schreinerstraße 48/49, 10247 Berlin, Germany. **Client:** City of Berlin, represented by the district of Friedrichshain-Kreuzberg. **Dragon design:** Freie Kunstschule Berlin. **Timber design:** Didaholz. **Completion:** 2001. **Materials:** wood, metal, ropes and sand. **Theme:** dragon land.

↑ | **Climbing trees with ropes and a net**
↓ | **Detail of wooden climbing structure**

↓ | **Springy tree trunk**

FANTASY   E.F.E.U. RIEDERER UND MÜNCH

↑ | Protrusions and recessions of the fence
← | Ropes for climbing over the boardwalk

DRAGON LAND

← | Slides on the side of the dragon
↓ | Rope web net

FANTASY | Monstrum

↑ | Ship Mary equipped with two slides

Rasmus Klump
Copenhagen

At Tivoli visitors can become part of the Rasmus Klump adventure. Rasmus and his friends have sailed their ship Mary onto an island and are climbing, jumping, swinging and splashing around it. Mary is resting on the side, which appears to be the hump of Rasmus' friend, the whale. Children can jump from rock to rock in the shallow water, climb the low-hanging ropes, and balance on the ropes in the shoreline, climb through barrels and play on the raft. With ice and blue water, Pingonisia is an ideal spot for the youngest children with tiny water spots, and gentle slopes. The seats close to the playing area are ideal for parents, who can easily observe their small children in the pleasantly enclosed area.

PROJECT FACTS **Address:** Vesterbrogade 3, 1630 Copenhagen V., Denmark. **Collaborating architects:** Jumana J. Brodersen / Jonathan Wright. **Client:** Tivoli Copenhagen. **Completion:** 2010. **Materials:** wood. **Theme:** Rasmus Klump stories.

↑ | **General view**
↓ | **Pingonisia playing area for younger children**

FANTASY   MONSTRUM

← | Ship Mary's interior
↓ | Ship Mary appears to be resting on a whale
→ | Submarine
↘ | Site plan

RASMUS KLUMP

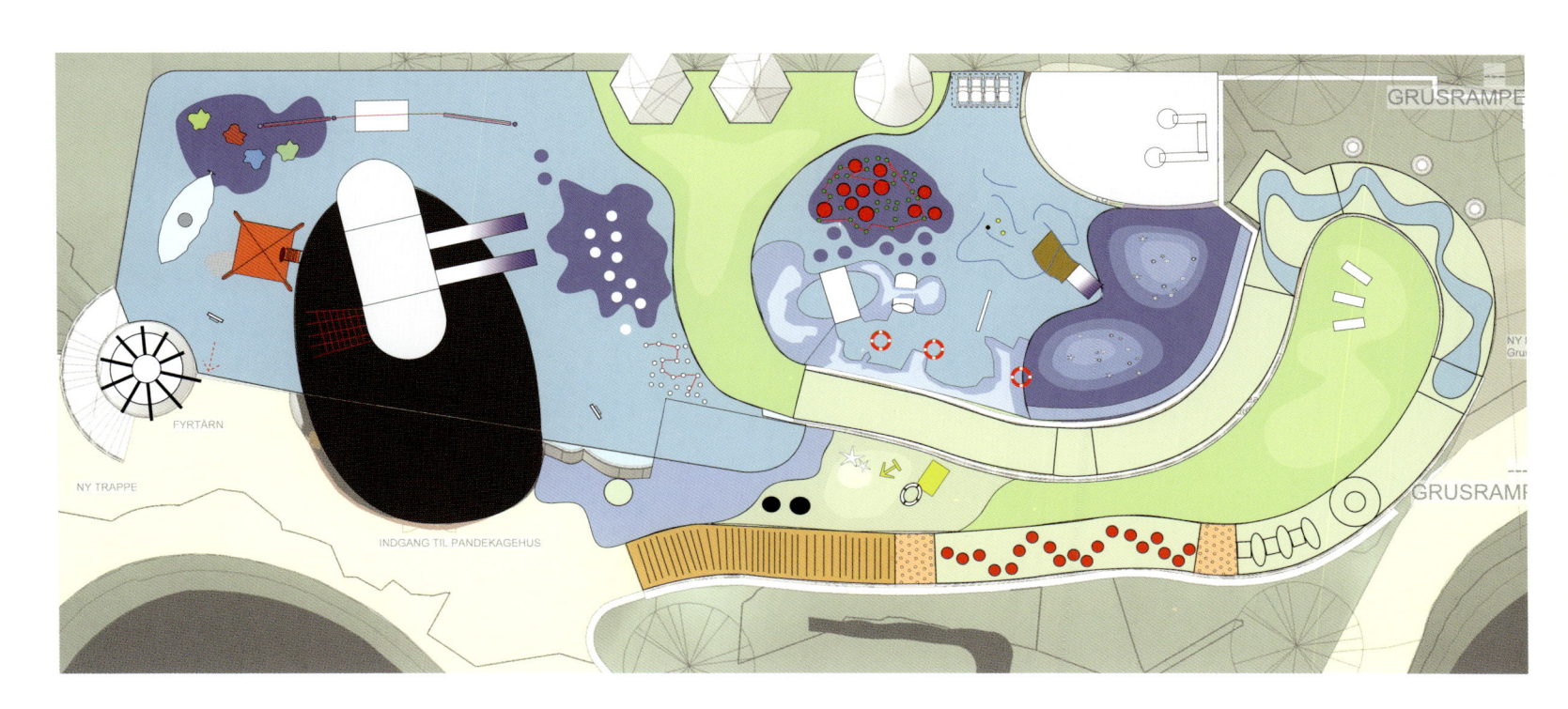

FYRTÅRN

NY TRAPPE

INDGANG TIL PANDEKAGEHUS

GRUSRAMPE

GRUSRAMP

FANTASY | Zimmer.Obst playground design

↑ | Colorful play structure and paths

Warnitzer Arches
Berlin

All constructional elements of the playground are made of black locust wood. The trunks are peeled to the heart wood, sanded, and color-treated. All poles for fixing to the ground are fitted with hot galvanized and powder-coated steel casings. They are inserted in 30x30x70 centimeters foundations made of concrete. The playful design is created by a colorful interplay of conically shaped sawed and dyed larch wood planks. A network of interlaced pedestal areas results in interesting play structures and play paths. Children with various motor skills can find their own way through it to the slide.

PROJECT FACTS **Address:** Warnitzer Straße, 10825 Berlin, Germany. **Client:** District of Lichtenberg, Berlin.
Landscape architects: Bode / Williams und Partner Landschaftsarchitektur. **Completion:** 2009.
Materials: locust, oak and larch wood. **Function:** large city walls.

↑ | **General view**
↓ | **Playground mirrors surrounding buildings**

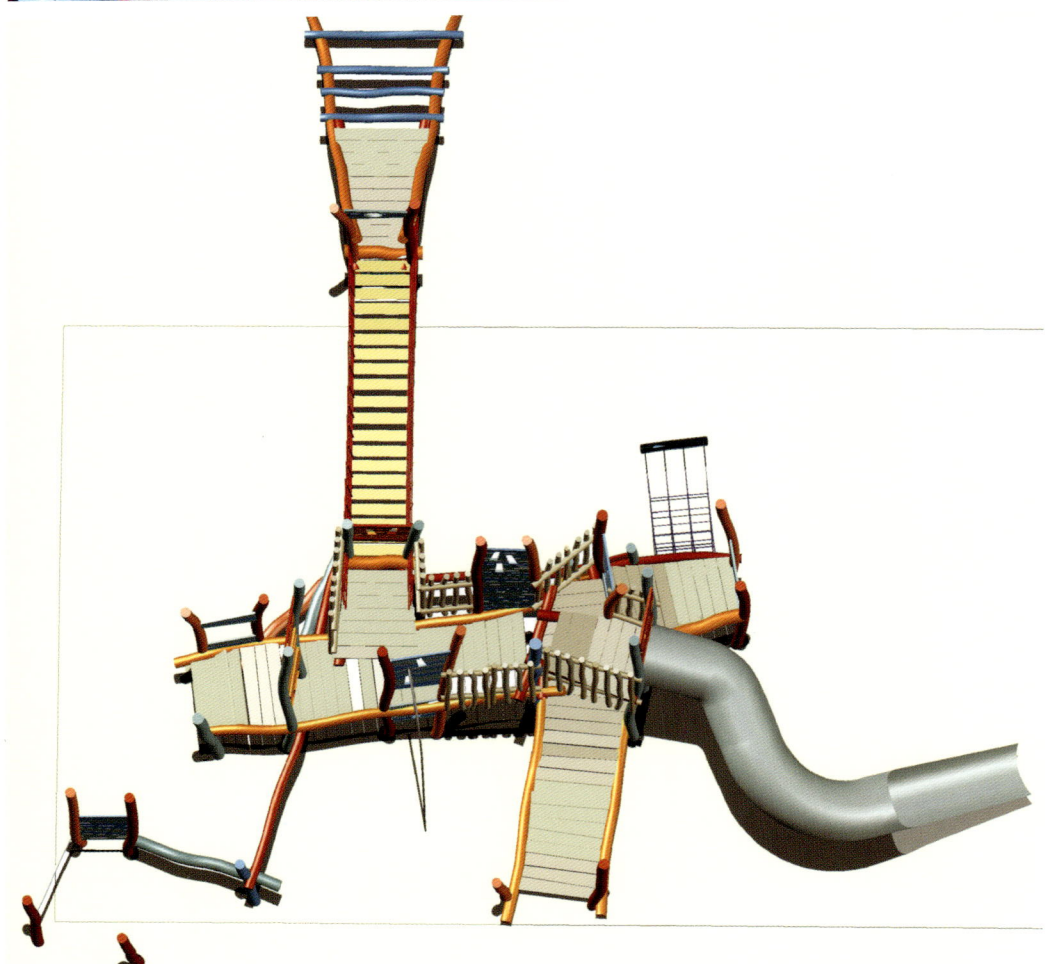

FANTASY   ZIMMER.OBST PLAYGROUND DESIGN

↑ | **Detail of colorful vertical and horizontal locust logs**
← | **Top view**

← | Climbing structure
↓ | Network of nested surfaces

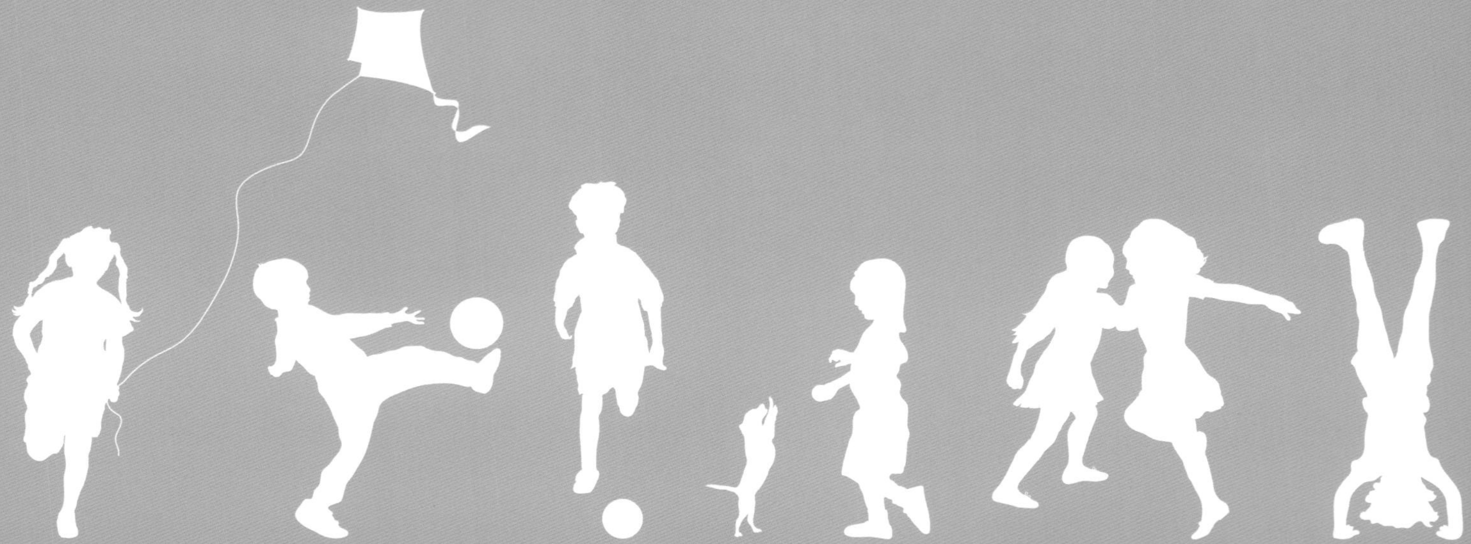

NATURE

NATURE | 24° Studio

↑ | Undulating wooden surface

Crater Lake
Kobe, Hyogo

The design of Crater Lake was influenced by the earthquake of 1995 that destroyed the built environment, sparing only the nature of Kobe. It consists of an undulating wooden landscape that provides a variation of settings with 360° views. Every surface may be utilized for seating and lying down with mobile seating stools placed at the center. The gentle hill surfaces invite people of all ages to interact with the landscape to play, relax, and socialize. After many ideas and materials were tested for the smooth and undulating forms, wood was chosen for its strong structural capacity, easy handling, and naturalness. The circular surface was divided into a number of radial parts, with the optimal number of 20 parts that were preassembled off-site and transported to the location.

PROJECT FACTS **Address:** Shiosai Koen, 1 Minatojima, Chuo-ku, Kobe, 650-0045 Hyogo, Japan. **Client:** Kobe Biennale Organization Committee / City of Kobe / Hyogo Prefecture. **Completion:** 2011. **Materials:** pine wood. **Theme:** mountain-, sea-, and cityscape.

↑ | Wooden surface to play and relax
↓ | Flexible stools

NATURE   24° STUDIO

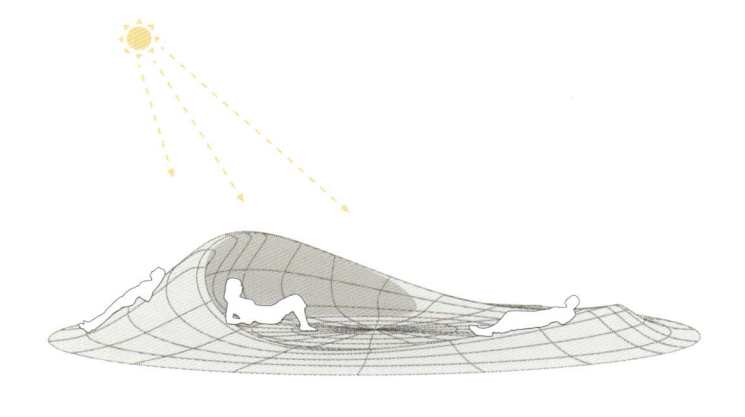

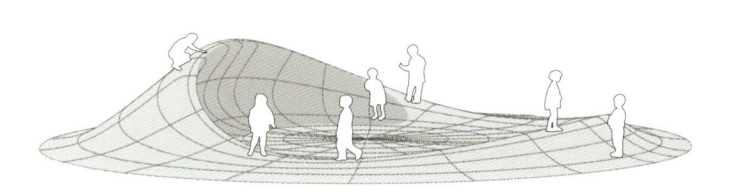

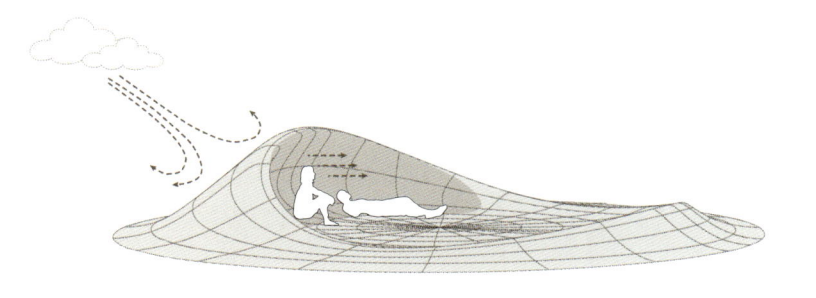

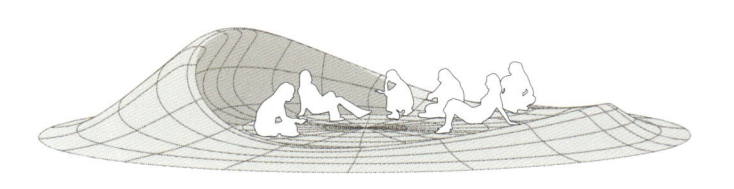

CRATER LAKE

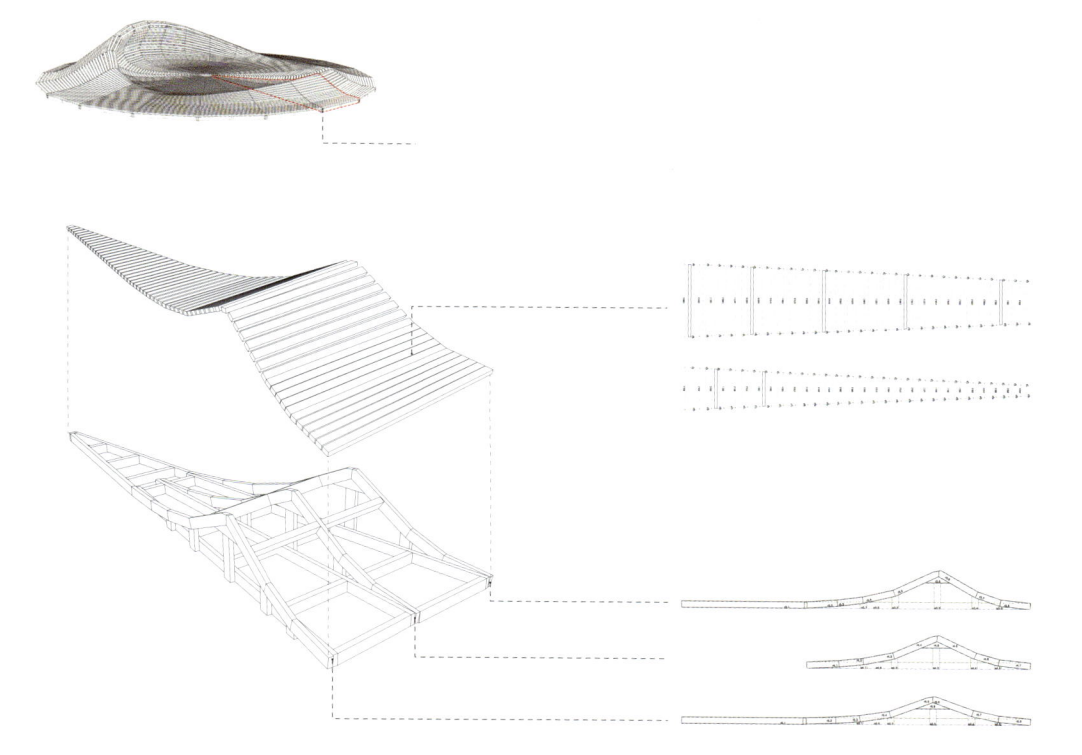

←← | View looking north towards Kobe City
↙↙ | Assembly diagram
← | Axonometry assembly diagram
↓ | Crater Lake used as playscape

NATURE | Carve

↑ | Child walking across wire mesh bridge

Vondelpark Canopy Walk
Amsterdam

The challenging playground design of the Vondelpark, suitable for all ages, consisted of a minimal building footprint, leaving the maximum ground space to meet the growing intensive use and offering enough capacity to all users. The playground is embedded in a wooded area and raised above the grounds, with a 75-meter long canopy walk. During summertime the canopy walk is hardly visible, it disappears between the leaves. There are different challenging ways to reach the path, climbing platforms, ropes, netting and tree trunks. The very transparent netting in the canopy walk, meters above ground level, makes children and adult experience height intensively. Addition of safety surfacing has been minimized; only at both ends of the walkway wood chips have been used.

PROJECT FACTS **Address:** Vondelpark, Amsterdam, The Netherlands. **Design collaboration:** City of Amsterdam, Quirijn Verhoog and Arno van Heemskerk. **Client:** the municipality of Amsterdam. **Completion:** 2010. **Materials:** wood and wire mesh. **Theme:** canopy walk.

↑ | View across canopy walk
↓ | Canopy construction

↓ | Inside bridge

NATURE   CARVE

↑ | Detail of bridge construction
← | Site plan

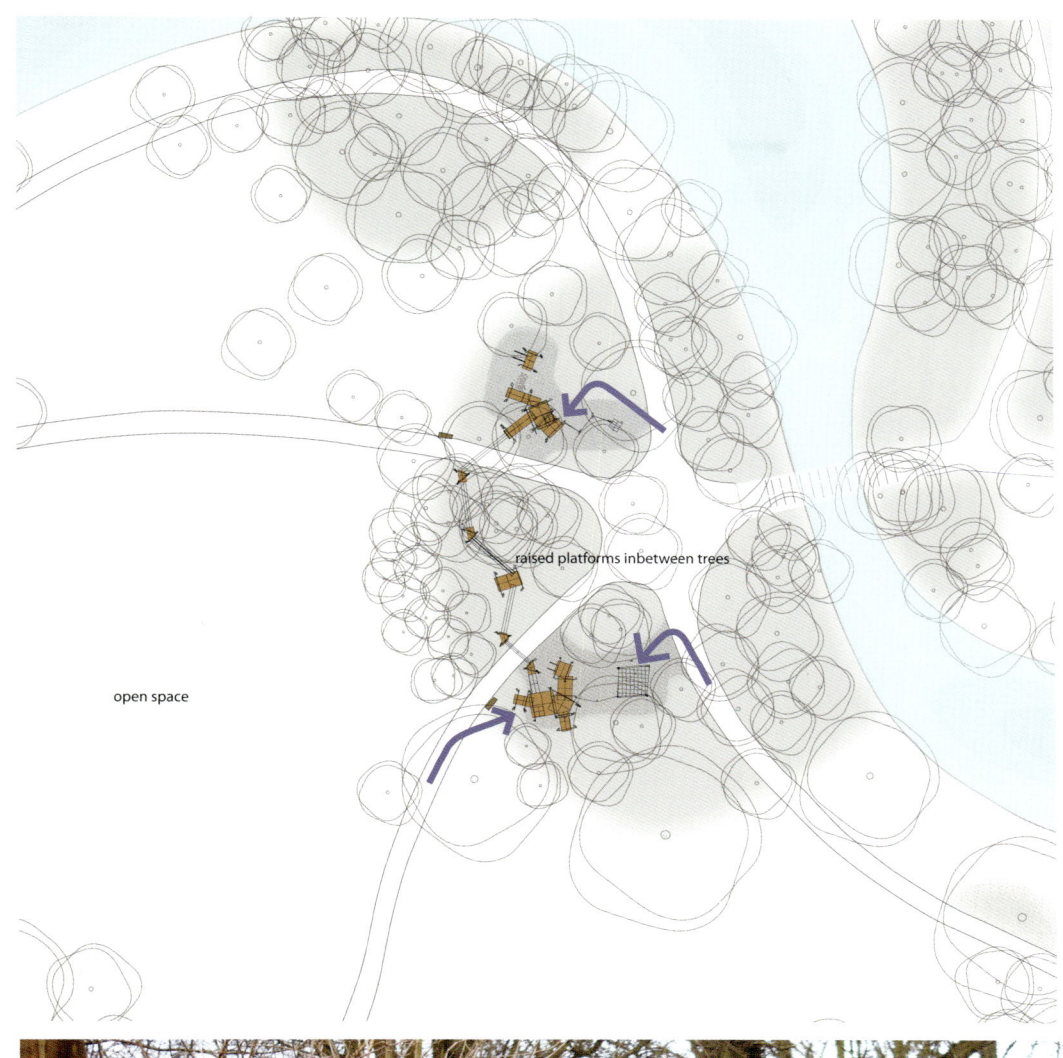

VONDELPARK CANOPY WALK

85

open space

raised platforms inbetween trees

← | Site plan
↓ | Hammock

NATURE | AMMA architecture de paysage

↑ | **Cables with balls run across poles**

Dry Cleaning II: "Fall into the Moon"

Grand-Métis, Quebec

The Nettoyage à sec (Dry cleaning) garden project was substantially altered and changed into Nettoyage à sec II with the theme of "fall into the moon". Under the concept of a healing and fun journey, it offers an invitation to escape into a lunar landscape. The surfaces were remodeled, colors redefined and the content renewed resulting in lunar craters, a monochrome landscape and references to the solar systems to encourage the discovery of space. The project adjusts the regenerative function of the gardens to the realities of the twenty-first century by combining a cleaning cycle with an escape to the moon.

PROJECT FACTS **Address:** Jardins de Metis International Garden Festival, 200, route 132, Grand-Métis, G0J 1Z0 Quebec, Canada. **Client:** Jardins de Metis / Reford Gardens. **Completion:** 2006. **Materials:** wood and sand. **Theme:** discovery of the space.

↑ | Detail of hanging chalk board
↓ | View across playground through opening

NATURE   AMMA ARCHITECTURE DE PAYSAGE

DRY CLEANING II: "FALL INTO THE MOON"

←← | Hanging strings appear as a clothes drying in a hanging rack
↑ | General view
← | Wooden pathway around playground

NATURE

geskes.hack
landscape architects

↑ | Colorful giant poles with water jets

Water Playground in Hemer
Hemer

As part of the Hemer 2010 Landesgartenschau (garden show) a water playground with a series of individually designed water play locations was created. The concept focuses on communication among the children with water bubbling among luscious tamarisks and willows. Hidden underground pump systems create showers and eddies in unexpected places. Huge greywacke boulders are in contrast to simple rectangular concrete water tables. The water forest contains colorful giant poles from whose height small water eddies or surge-like jets of water emerge.

PROJECT FACTS **Address:** Ostenschlahstraße 15, 58675 Hemer, Germany. **Client:** Landesgartenschau, Hemer. **Completion:** 2010. **Materials:** concrete, greywacke boulders, gravel, rubber and water. **Function:** communication among the children with water bubbling.

↑ | Greywacke boulders with hidden water system
↓ | General view

↑ | Children play around giant colorful poles

NATURE GESKES.HACK LANDSCAPE ARCHITECTS

← | Concrete table with water faucet
↓ | Greywacke boulders shooting water

WATER PLAYGROUND IN HEMER

↑ | Site plan
← | Children play on concrete water table

NATURE

Kunder³
Landschaftsarchitektur

↖↖ | Play towers connected by a metal tunnel
↖ | New structures
↑ | Site plan

Tapachtal Playground
Stuttgart

The restructuring of the playground with three sections began in 2007 incorporating the wishes of all involved parties, including children and youths. In addition to the restructuring and renovation of the playground, the adjacent playing field and the existing skating facility was turned into a youth center in line with the master plan. After the plan was agreed upon, construction work began, substantially supported by construction teams of the involved youths. On two weekends, they were allowed to contribute to the creation of "their" youth center under the expert supervision of the implementing company.

PROJECT FACTS   **Address:** Abstatter Straße, 70437 Stuttgart, Germany. **Client:** Garten-, Friedhofs- und Forstamt der Landeshauptstadt Stuttgart. **Completion:** 2010. **Materials:** wood, stones, metal and sand. **Theme:** restructuring playground.

↑ | **Different playing surfaces**   ↓ | **Seating area**
↓ | **Seating benches step up to landscape**

NATURE — ANNABAU Architektur und Landschaft

↑ | Suspended net walkway loop

Sculptural Playground
Wiesbaden

Located in a formerly neglected area overlooking the historic center of the city of Wiesbaden in Germany, the Schulberg "sculptural playground" offers a very child-friendly environment. Accommodating the wishes of children and parents, it is big enough to hold even the most active kid's attention for several visits. Designed by Berlin-based ANNABAU Architektur und Landschaft, the pentagon-shaped play area mirrors the city's historic shape. The playground consists of three elements: a suspended net walkway loop supported by two undulating lengths of stainless-steel pipe; an artificial landscape created inside the loop; and a wide boulevard with benches outside the loop.

PROJECT FACTS **Location:** Wiesbaden, Germany. **Structural design:** Niehues Winkler Ingenieure. **Client:** Office for parks, agriculture and forestry, Wiesbaden. **Completion:** 2011. **Materials:** EPDM rubber, steel-pipe, net. **Theme:** endless possibilities of playing in the loop.

↑ | Walkway net follows the sculptural piece
↓ | View across playground

NATURE   ANNABAU ARCHITEKTUR UND LANDSCHAFT

↖ | Children jump across walkway net
↑ | Children crawl across the net
← | Site plan
↗ | Sections
→ | Child walks on the stainless steel pipe

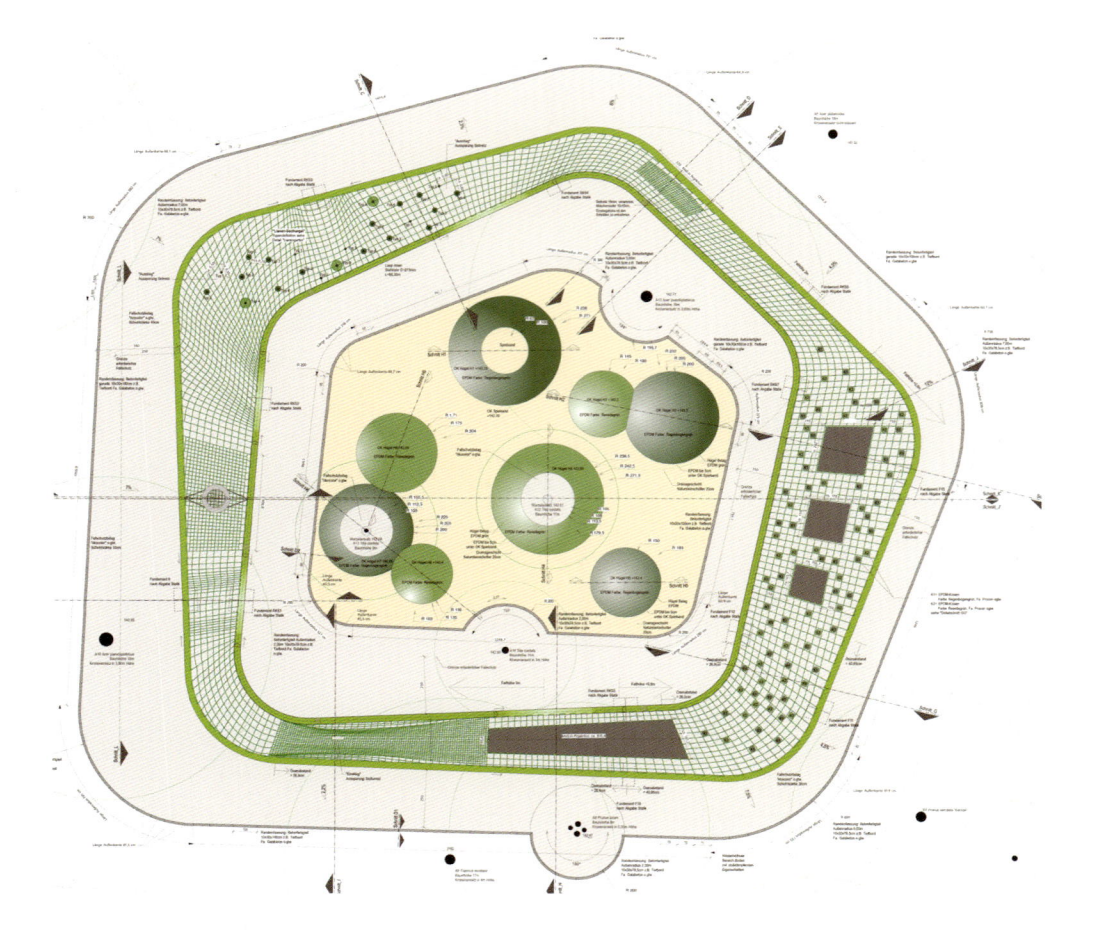

SCULPTURAL PLAYGROUND

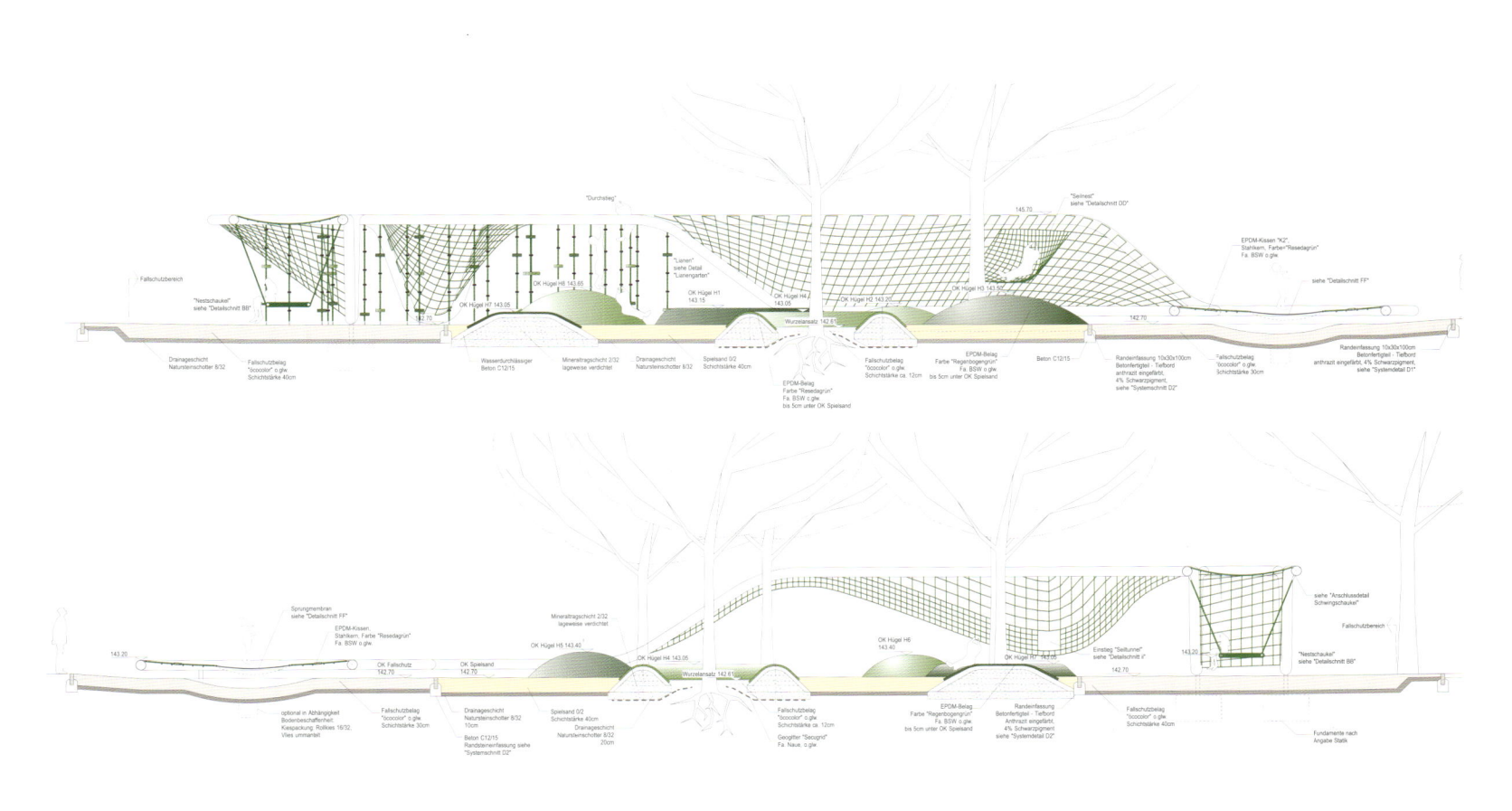

NATURE · Aspect Studios

↑ | The water play area with sand pits and slides

Darling Quarter
Sydney, NSW

Aspect Studios has designed a new public precinct and urban play space in Sydney's Darling Harbor. At over 4,000 square meters it is the largest play space in Sydney's CBD and will increase the popularity of the district, the most visited destination in Australia. It offers an adventurous and highly interactive play experience based on the Australian climate. The water play area includes interactive water elements such as sluice gates, hand pumps, and an "Archimedes" screw,' which draws water up and channels it back into a myriad of sculptural concrete streams. The stainless steel elements promote social interaction and learning while referencing the industrial history of the site. There is also a "dry" playground with sand pits, a flying fox, giant climbing frames, and group slides.

PROJECT FACTS **Address:** Darling Drive, Sydney NSW 2000, Australia. **Client:** Sydney Harbour Foreshore Authority. **Lighting designer:** Speirs + Major. **Other creatives:** Lend Lease / FJMT / Waterforms International. **Completion:** 2011. **Materials:** pine wood. **Theme:** references the site's former industrial uses and indigenous landscape.

↑ | Junior slides and sand pit with mounded topography
↓ | The highly popular "flying fox"

↓ | Children trying to release the slice gates in the water play area

NATURE　　　　　　　　　　ASPECT STUDIOS

← | Precast concrete "boulders" provide seating and site interpretation
↓ | Views across the pedestrian boulevard to the water play area

DARLING QUARTER

↑ | Site plan
← | Table tennis

NATURE | CPG Australia

↑ | **Volcano slides and dry creek bed**

Rooke Reserve
Truganina

Rooke Reserve is a new 15,000 square meters playground centrally located within a new residential development in Truganina, approximately 20 kilometers west of the Melbourne CBD. Its location and design provide clearly defined pedestrian and bicycle connections to surrounding residential neighborhoods, the Federation Trail Bicycle Network, Truganina South Primary School, Arndell District Open Space, Community Center and Kindergarten, and Skeleton Creek. Play is central to the design intent of Rooke Reserve, with both its structure and setting designed to facilitate the specific requirements for 2–5 year old play, 5–w12 year old play and access for general play. Whilst structured play elements highlight specific play zones, they also act to trigger investigation of the sites' texture, topography and materials.

PROJECT FACTS **Address:** Federation Boulevard, Truganina VIC 3029, Australia. **Client:** Devine Group. **Completion:** 2010. **Materials:** timber, concrete, EPDM rubber, rock (site sourced basalt), warm season grass, native planting. **Theme:** volcanos.

↑ | Lava flow area with slides for 2–5 year old children
↓ | Informal seating also provides play element

NATURE CPG AUSTRALIA

↑ | Child climbing up the "volcano" slide
← | Site plan

ROOKE RESERVE

↑ | Sketch
← | Street view of Rooke Reserve

NATURE | Erect Architecture

↑ | Recycled materials

Kilburne Grange Park Play Center and Park
London

The site of the adventure playground is the remainder of a Victorian Arboretum. Its theme is playing in and around trees. The play park consists of new topographies, landscapes and site-specific climbing structures. Different scales, speeds, uses, types of inhabitation and play as well as materials and moods are carefully arranged. Children can experience different seasons or even hours of the day. The dense adventure structure plays with the characters of the trees, telling their stories. The structure is complex with small spaces of varied materials. A series of recycled doors quotes domesticity but also offers routes through the perpetually changing expanding and contracting spaces. Different degrees of secrecy provide various vantage points into the park.

PROJECT FACTS **Address:** Kilburn Grange Park, Messina Avenue, Camden, London NW6 4LD, United Kingdom. **Client:** London Borough of Camden. **Artist:** Ashley McCormick. **Completion:** 2010. **Materials:** timber, net and found objects. **Theme:** trees.

↑ | Different climbing routes
↓ | Top view of path down to the park

NATURE   ERECT ARCHITECTURE

↑ | Detail of lookout point
← | Exterior view of play center
↗ | Play structures wrap around the trees
→ | Floor plan

KILBURN GRANGE PARK PLAY CENTER AND PARK

NATURE | geskes.hack
landscape architects

↑ | View to volcano from "desert land"

Atoll Playground
Schwerin

The nature garden is one of the seven gardens of the BUGA Schwerin 2009. This landscape is a piece of untouched and valuable nature in the middle of town. For this reason, only boardwalks and tree trunk paths are accessible. At the center of the nature garden lies the Atoll playground. In cooperation with the Gisbert Baarmann workshop for wood design, landscapes with climb-on volcanoes, giant frogs and sound sculptures were created. Three atolls – desert land, fire land, and swamp land – provide play opportunities for different age groups and requirements. Climbing sculptures resembling volcanoes glow like red lava from a distance, while scattered rocks resemble cooled lava streams.

PROJECT FACTS **Address:** Eckdrift 43–45, 19061 Schwerin, Germany. **Client:** Bundesgartenschau Schwerin. **Timber design:** Gisbert Baarmann. **Completion:** 2009. **Materials:** wood and tartan. **Theme:** Tierra del Fuego, desert, swamp.

↑ | **Child jumps inside small "volcano"**
↓ | **Lava stones**

↓ | **Tree trunk paths**

NATURE   GESKES.HACK LANDSCAPE ARCHITECTS

↑ | Children climb up the "volcano"-like playground
← | Site plan

ATOLL PLAYGROUND

115

← | Looking up from the inside "volcano"
↓ | Inside the "volcano"

NATURE | plancontext landschaftsarchitektur

↑ | **Field Loop playground**

Playgrounds of the National Garden Show Norderstedt
Norderstedt

The specific identities of the existing different types of landscapes at the Norderstedt city park were enhanced for the Landesgartenschau (National garden show) of 2011. This resulted in three parks within a park: the Lake Park, the Forest Park and the Field Park. The three sections are connected by an enveloping sculptural series of promenades, the "Loop". Three different play areas were developed for the three sections with a uniform overall concept. They are called the Water Loop, the Forest Loop and the Field Loop, each matched to the location and requirements of different age groups.

PROJECT FACTS **Address:** Stadtpark, 22846 Norderstedt, Germany. **Client:** Stadtpark Norderstedt. **Garden show concept:** Büro Kiefer. **Engineer:** iwf Ingenieurbüro for Water Technology. **Completion:** 2011. **Materials:** wood, stainless steel case, protective covering of plastic, sand and river gravel. **Theme:** water, forest and field loop.

↑ | Water Loop playground
↓ | Forest Loop playground

NATURE PLANCONTEXT LANDSCHAFTSARCHITEKTUR

↖ | Sheep series in Field Loop
↑ | Rope bridge in Forest Loop
← | Dancing sheep in Field Loop

PLAYGROUNDS OF THE NATIONAL GARDEN SHOW NORDERSTEDT

↑ | "Straw bale house" in Field Loop
← | Water Loop, site plan

NATURE | Jane Hutton & Adrian Blackwell

↑ | **General view of structure**

Dymaxion Sleep
Grand-Métis, Quebec

Dymaxion Sleep is a structure of nets suspended over a field of aromatic plants. Rather than walking through the garden, visitors lie on top of it, translating the typically solitary experience of a garden into a public event. An unfolded icosahedron holds the nets, formed of twenty steel triangles. Each triangle is large enough to support a single outstretched body, an intertwined pair, or a pile-up of people. The structure is anchored to a timber footing, which traces the diagram of the icosahedron on the soil. Mints, lemon geranium, lavender and fennel are planted below, mimicking the structure's topography and defining scented territories in which to relax. The form of each layer of this double surface, planting, and nets is based on Buckminster Fuller's Dymaxion World Map.

PROJECT FACTS **Address:** Jardins de Metis International Garden Festival, 200, route 132, Grand-Métis, G0J 1Z0 Quebec, Canada. **Client:** Jardins de Metis / Reford Gardens. **Other creatives:** Walter Blackwell / Carole Courtois & Dany Fillion. **Completion:** 2009. **Materials:** steel, wood, netting and planting (mints, lavender, fennel, pelargonium). **Theme:** an unfolded icosahedron, Buckminster Fuller's Dymaxion World Map.

↑ | **Lying on structure's net**
↓ | **Unfolded icosahedron structure above garden**

NATURE   JANE HUTTON & ADRIAN BLACKWELL

↑ | Detail of structure and net
← | Child playing on inclined net surface

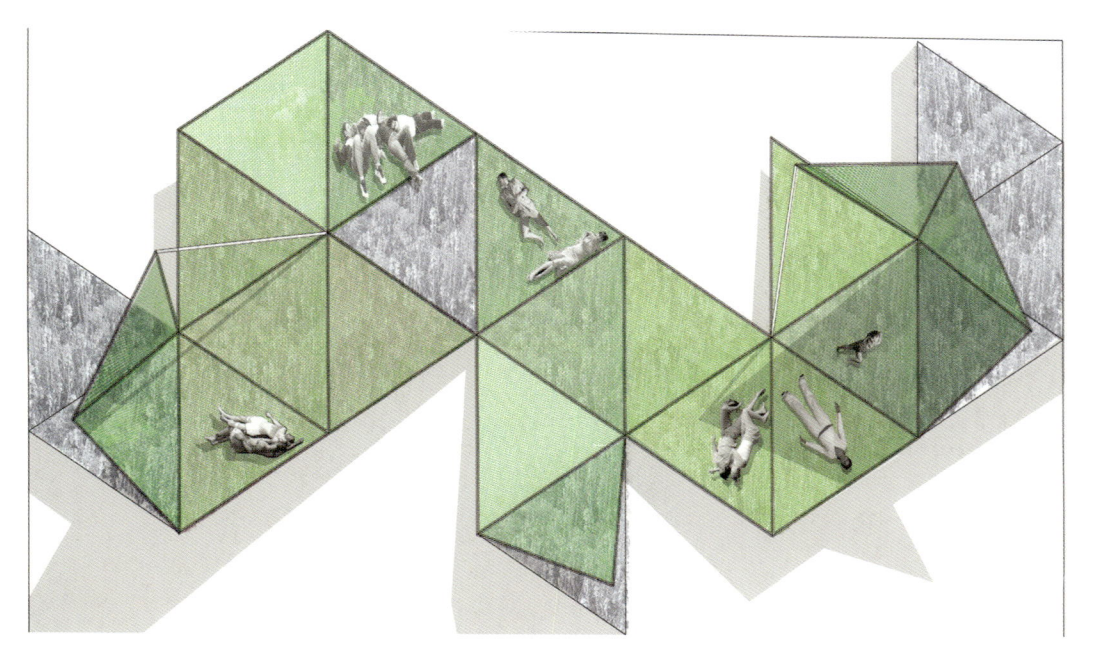

DYMAXION SLEEP   123

← | Icosahedron diagram
↓ | Children playing across the structure

NATURE | Rainer Schmidt Landschaftsarchitekten

↖↖ | Creek running through the park
↑↑ | Strolling through the park
↖ | Site plan
↑ | View from the lake to the south

Heights Park Killesberg
Stuttgart

The design blends two themes that dominate the Killesberg area – soft, natural landscapes and stone quarries as hard topographic elements. This results in a landscape with its own story to tell – the hard shapes of a quarry topography change with the years, becoming more rounded until they turn into a soft landscape covered in soil and greenery. Meadows are the themes linking all sections of the park. Main paths, a network of bicycle paths, and small strolling tracks cross the hilly landscape. This results in a lively soft playground topography of meadow cushions that create a harmonious whole. Running and jumping over varied landscapes is very attractive to children of all ages. In addition to this comprehensive play area, the hills feature several smaller play areas for different ages.

PROJECT FACTS **Location:** Killesberg, Stuttgart, Germany. **Client:** City of Stuttgart, Garden, Cemetery and Forestry Office. **Landscape architect:** Rainer Schmidt Landschaftsarchitekten in cooperation with Pfrommer + Roeder Freie Landschaftsarchitekten. **Completion:** 2012. **Materials:** meadow structure. **Theme:** moving scenery as latitude.

↑ | **Park's topography**
↓ | **Topography of hills, meadows game**

NATURE | Carve

↑ | Twin play towers with slides

Vondelpark Towers
Amsterdam

The two playing towers were designed for the playground in the Vondelpark at the "Amstelveenseweg" entrance. It is based on the architecture of the adjacent "de Vondeltuin" pavilion. The footprint of the towers connects two circular existing playgrounds, which were built in the early sixties by the Dutch architect Aldo van Eyck. An opening splits the volume into two equal parts to keep a line of sight on the colonial buildings. This allowed the creation of two different playable interiors. One is based on platforms from which the lower slide can be reached. The other one has a challenging rope circuit leading to a transparent high bridge connected to the big slide.

PROJECT FACTS **Address:** Van Campenvaart. The Hague, The Netherlands. **Client:** District Zuid of Amsterdam. **Collaborating architects:** Quirijn Verhoog and Arno van Heemskerk. **Completion:** 2010. **Materials:** wood, metal, ropes and sand. **Theme:** based on the architecture of the adjacent pavilion "de Vondeltuin".

↑ | Bridge connecting the towers
↓ | Detail of sliding tube perforating the tower

NATURE CARVE

VONDELPARK TOWERS

↖↖ | View towards playable tower interior
←← | Tower interior with climbing ropes
↙↙ | General view
← | View up towards connecting bridge
↓ | Conceptual drawing

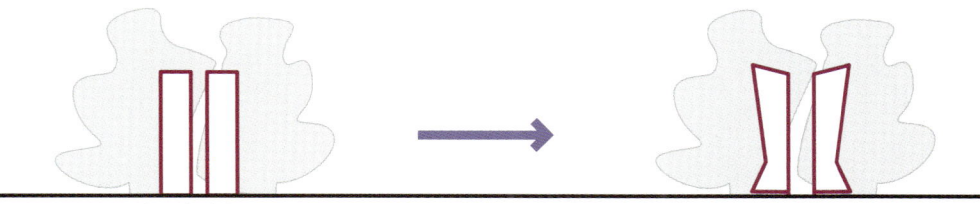

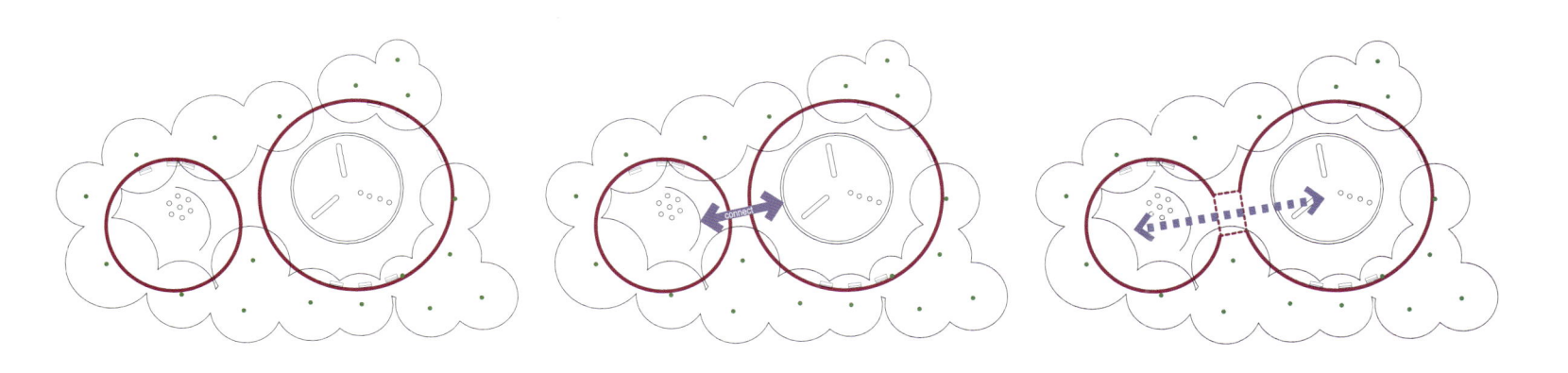

NATURE | Jeavons Landscape Architects

↑ | Lookout over playground

Stud Park Playground
Rowville

The project consists of an accessible and socially inclusive regional play space for children and adults regardless of their age or physical ability. Visitors with disabilities can play, supervise their children, and participate in social activities on an equal basis. The natural environment is an important element and the playground is carefully integrated into the landscape. The design extends the existing terrain, using it as a linking element to provide wheelchair accessibility to all elevated areas and set a framework for the climbing and sliding elements and lookouts. The mounds form three-dimensional spaces with social and interactive play corners, and many nooks and crannies that children can discover suitable to their individual needs.

PROJECT FACTS Address: Stud Road / Fulham Road, Rowville VIC 3178, Australia. Client: City of Knox. Sound artist: Herb Jercher. Completion: 2008. Materials: metal, wood and sand. Theme: accessible for adults and children.

↑ | Children playing on tower with an interactive tilting deck
↓ | Tower evoking the form of a rural water tank

↓ | Detail of accessible elevated deck with viewing port through to the ground

← | **Elevated wheelchair accessible slide**
↓ | **Structures interweave into mounded terrain**

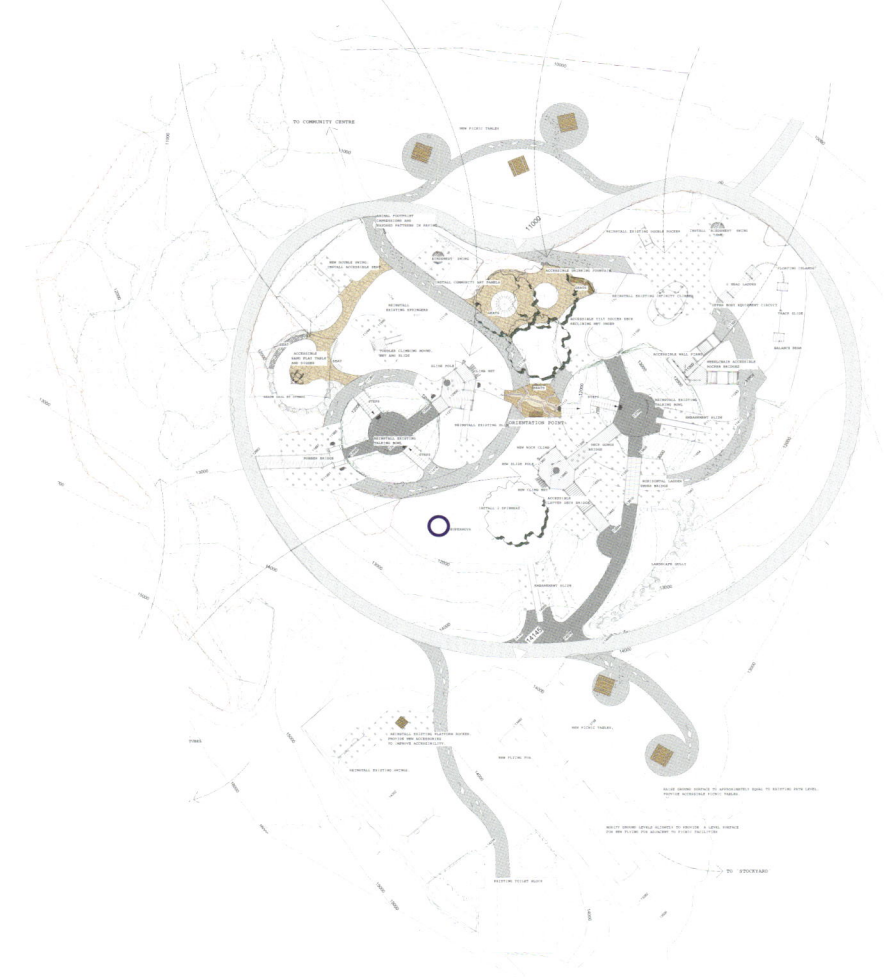

STUD PARK PLAYGROUND

↑ | Under deck activities: sound drums and wheelchair accessible push-pin game
← | Community artworks framing central gathering space

NATURE | LAND-I archicolture

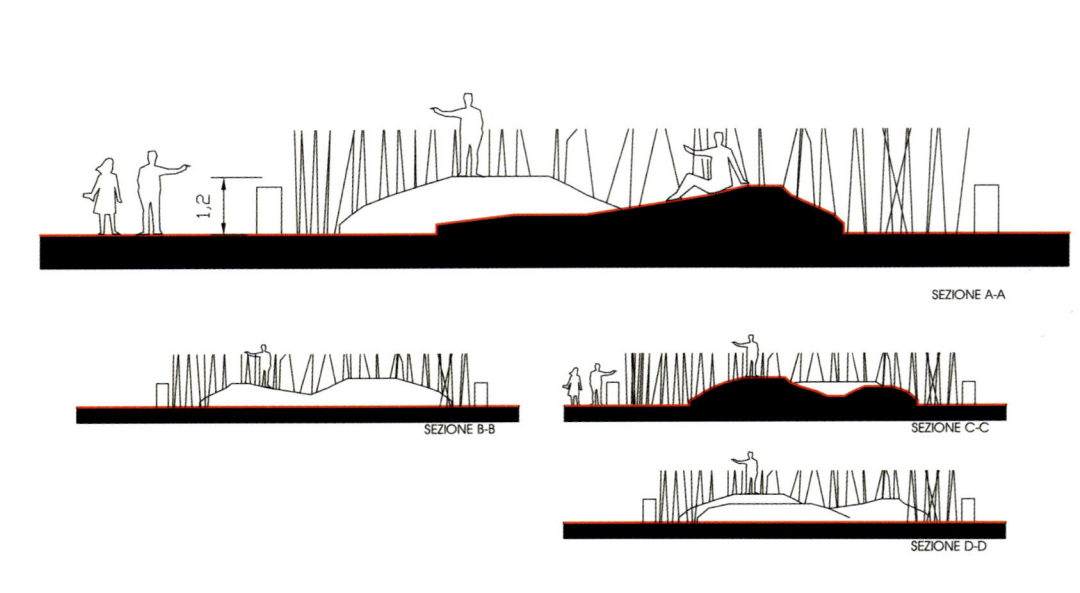

↖↖ | Stone extended as a landscape for playing
↖ | Sections
↑ | Planted flowers

Stone's Throw Playground
Sonoma, CA

Similarly to pop art, an object was blown to surreal dimensions for this design. In this case an arbitrarily chosen but unique stone of a specific landscape, a beach on the Mediterranean. Its de-contextualization and placement on an urban lawn was a necessary intermediate step to define its identity. It was then transformed into a landscape to be experienced by visitors. "Informed" through images that depict the stone in its original and transitory environment, they close the conceptual circle by actively and emotionally living the site. The "opening" theme of the festival is reflected twice in the garden installation – physically by planted holes in the stone, creating "life pockets" in its lifeless surface, and more abstractly by the visitors on an imaginary voyage through space and time.

PROJECT FACTS **Address:** CornerStone Garden Festival, 23570 Arnold Drive, 95476 Sonoma, CA, USA. **Client:** Cornerstone Sonoma. **Completion:** 2004. **Materials:** concrete. **Theme:** a stone as a livable landscape.

↑ | **Perforated stone landscape**
↓ | **Floor plan**

↓ | **Stone detail**

NATURE | Martha Schwartz Partners

↑ | **Metal slides**

Monte Laa Central Park
Vienna

The Central Park is the heart and focal point of the housing project Gartenstadt Laaerberg. The overall premise for the design was to establish the park as a separate, strong entity within the project, providing a striking visual identity and an unforgettable experience. Martha Schwartz Partners proposed a configuration of elongated sculptural landforms, lines of columnar trees and bands of different materials that work together to emphasize the linear quality of the park. These elements are of the same geometric and formal arrangement as the overall layout of the Gartenstadt. The most active zone in the park is deliberately located close to the school with an easy connection to the school yard as to invite use by the children. The ramp and its surroundings provide play facilities for children with the landform paved in asphalt for optimal use by skaters and skate boarders. The end of the landform houses a children's play fountain.

PROJECT FACTS **Address:** Emil-Fucik Gasse, Vienna, Austria. **Client:** PORR. **Completion:** 2002. **Materials:** metal, concrete, stones, wood and grass. **Theme:** elongated sculptural landforms.

↑ | Linear park, follows its landscape
↓ | Play fountain

↓ | Grass slide

NATURE　　　　　　　　　　　MARTHA SCHWARTZ PARTNERS

↑ | View to linear park with slides
← | Detail metal slide

MONTE LAA CENTRAL PARK

← | Stairs
↓ | Sand box playing area

NATURE | plancontext
landschaftsarchitektur

↑ | View down to climbing net

Atlantis Playground
Berlin

The Atlantis playground in Berlin Kreuzberg was created with the intense involvement of the neighborhood's children. In response to their frequently stated desire for water, an underwater world theme was adopted. The "Neptune temple" combines equipment for sliding, climbing and swinging. A huge "climbing octopus" offers play opportunities primarily aimed at older children. Suspended on springs, the "surf shark" trains motor development. A poured concrete "whale" with a slide and waterspout became the favorite of the youngest visitors. Surrounded by columns and a blue fence with fish decorations, the adjacent playing field became an "aquarium" suitable to the theme.

PROJECT FACTS **Address:** Wrangelstraße 11, 10997 Berlin, Germany. **Client:** district of Friedrichshain-Kreuzberg, Berlin. **Completion:** 2010. **Materials:** wood, steel, shotcrete, impact protection layer made of plastic and sand. **Theme:** underwater world.

↑ | **Shark surfing, climbing octopus and "Temple of Neptune"**
↓ | **"Aquarium": blue field**

↓ | **Ground trampolines in the "sandbar"**

NATURE PLANCONTEXT LANDSCHAFTSARCHITEKTUR

ATLANTIS PLAYGROUND

↖↖ | "Temple of Neptune"
←← | Whale with climbing hold grips
↑ | View to climbing octopus from below
← | Site plan

NATURE

Rainer Schmidt
Landschaftsarchitekten

↑ | General view

BUGA
Munich

The BUGA park is subtly becoming the central part of the 2005 Bundesgartenschau (Federal Garden Show) of Munich – the organic as the structural basic pattern of all types of flora is the dominating theme of the central exhibition areas. The presentation of different perspectives, the micro and the macro, is the recurring theme with different expressions throughout the entire garden show premises. Microscopic plant structures in various dimensions were the inspiration for the design of the "Gärten der Potenzen" ("Gardens of magnitude"). Orange paths with rubber covering extend across the lawns. Lawn hills with different heights provide a lively play area for children of all ages. Running, bouncing, jumping – all are possible on the colorful rubber cover and the soft meadow rises.

PROJECT FACTS　**Address:** Messestadt Riem, Munich, Germany. **Client:** Federal Garden Show of Munich. **Completion:** 2005. **Materials:** rubber flooring and lawn. **Theme:** hill grass landspcape.

↑ | Aerial view
↓ | Detail of lawn hills

↓ | Bird's-eye view of the gardens

NATURE RAINER SCHMIDT LANDSCHAFTSARCHITEKTEN

BUGA

←← | Lawn hill with orange paths
↑ | Orange path for running
↙ | Floor plan

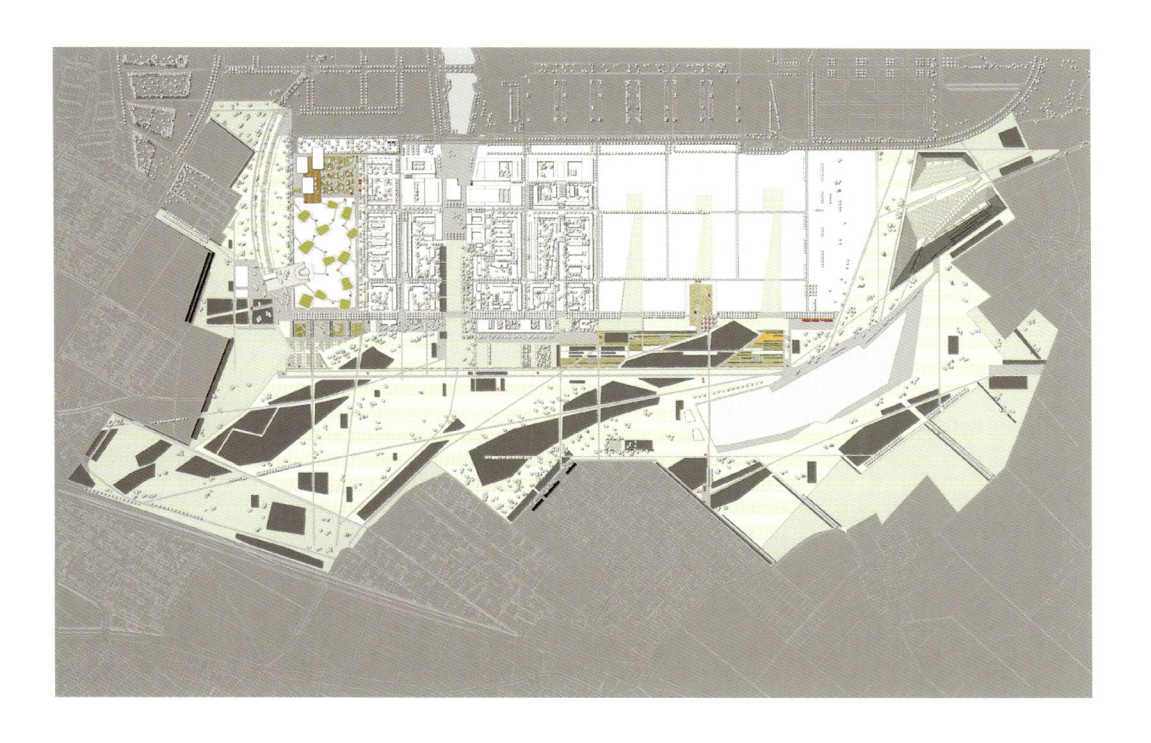

NATURE | RS+

↑ | Internal wooden bench becomes a fence in the exterior

Water Playground
Tychy

The water playground was merged into the landscape, with the location and contour of the basin matching the existing trees. RS+ used exotic wood on the floor in front of entrance and on benches around the basin. The basin had to be secured against unwanted animals and people, taking into account the effect of fences on the landscape. Wooden fencing was used resembling shifted sine waves, creating delicate characteristic elements, which separate the basin. Technical rooms were covered with grass to minimize their impact on the landscape. Colorful aquatic toys were selected with different functions. In addition, a zone for younger children with milder foaming water toys was created. In the evening, the playground becomes a fountain with programmable multicolored LED illumination.

PROJECT FACTS **Address:** Parkowa, Paprocany, Tychy, Poland. **Client:** Tychy Town Council. **Water engineering:** ARRAS B Sp. z o.o. **Construction company:** PW-2. **Completion:** 2011. **Materials:** exotic wood, EPDM rubber and stainless steel. **Theme:** water.

↑ | Colorful water playground
↓ | Fountain with LED illumination

↓ | Giant flowers shoot water

NATURE RS+

SIDE VIEW

WATER PLAYGROUND

←← | Illuminated playground by night
↙↙ | Floor plan and elevation
← | Curvilinear seating area
↓ | Water playground follows the water basin

NATURE | Space2place

↑ | Wood stump for climbing

Garden City Play Environment
Richmond

The park is an organic, flowing space with a setting that invokes the natural world and reflects the regional character of the Pacific Northwest. Interaction with elements and items found in nature such as insects, water, streams, ponds, sand, salvaged tree limbs and ribbons of perennial vegetation introduces city kids to larger natural systems. The Garden City play environment is unique because it responds to its distinctive context, develops awareness for natural systems and provides a rich diversity of play and learning experiences that absorb children for hours. The process has stimulated new design approaches for children's play areas. Concepts such as nature-based play and integration of play with public spaces are changing society's perception of traditional playgrounds.

PROJECT FACTS **Address:** Garden City Park, Richmond BC, Canada. **Client:** City of Richmond. **Wood artist:** Warren Brubacher. **Completion:** 2008. **Materials:** wood, steel, concrete, water, sand, plants, rubber and stone. **Theme:** nature-based play.

↑ | Water channel runs around playground
↓ | Walking on steel poles

NATURE SPACE2PLACE

← | Site plan
↓ | Stepping stones

GARDEN CITY PLAY ENVIRONMENT

↑ | Sand and water play
← | Water channel and weir

NATURE | Stoss Landscape Urbanism

↑↑ | **Three-dimensional rubber surface landscape hills and goal bumpers in trees**
↖ | **Built-in landscape hills**
↑ | **Site plan**

Safe Zone
Grand-Métis

The design makes playful use of products designed for dangerous locations: poured rubber surfaces, plastic warning strips, traction mats, goal post bumpers, with everyday materials of subway platforms, sidewalks, playgrounds and sports fields are positioned in a provocative new way. Government safety regulations and the materials used for them are used differently, opening up possibilities for free, uninhibited play and exploration. The garden's main surface, poured-in-place rubber, is applied three-dimensionally, allowing for spatial differentiation, creative play, and movement among the trees. While the garden is synthetic, 80% of its materials are recycled or salvaged. The surface is also permeable, allowing water to penetrate it to irrigate tree roots and recharge the water table.

PROJECT FACTS **Address:** Jardins de Métis International Garden Festival, 200, route 132, Grand-Métis, G0J 1Z0 Quebec, Canada. **Client:** Jardins de Métis / Reford Gardens. **Completion:** 2009. **Materials:** rubber mulch surfacing, vinyl-covered foam pad, polyurethane-based, flexible paint, trees and rocks. **Theme:** safe zone.

↑ | Playing among trees in rubber surface
↓ | Running across the "plastic warning strips"

↓ | "Plastic warning strip" surface

NATURE | ver.de landschaftsarchitektur

↑ | Oversized apples in the meadow

"Im Gefilde" Playground
Munich

The "Im Gefilde" green area is designed as a sweeping meadow valley with a variety of play areas. The "fruit crates" are play areas for small children based on wooden crates embedded in traditional orchards also featuring oversized apples. The "garden plott" with its modeled turf is designed like an oversized garden bed with play elements suspended from large horizontal or vertical stalks of chives. The "tree plot" shaped like a giant leaf consists of the naturally grown stems of Black Locust trees with suspended climbing nets.

PROJECT FACTS **Location:** Putzbrunner Straße/Arnold-Sommerfeld-Straße, Munich, Germany. **Client:** City of Munich, Baureferat Gartenbau. **Oversized apples' design:** Gisbert Baarmann. **Completion:** 2006. **Materials:** black locust logs, oak and Douglas fir planks, galvanized steel, stainless steel. **Theme:** fruit crates, tree and garden plots.

↑ | Orchard with different fruit crates
↓ | Construction of the fruit crates

↓ | One of the three orchards visualized

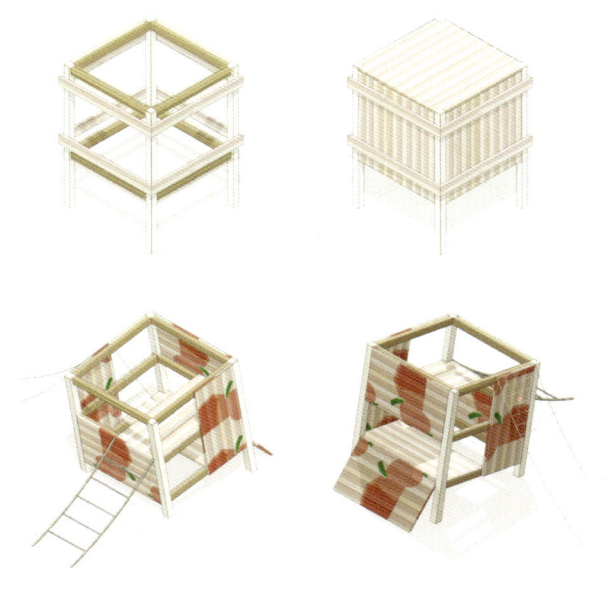

NATURE   VER.DE LANDSCHAFTSARCHITEKTUR

↑ | Garden plot as oversized bed visualized
← | Wooden surfaces wrap around tree trunks in garden plot

"IM GEFILDE" PLAYGROUND

← | Children climb up to the highest point
↓ | Tree plot with climbing nets

NATURE | Rainer Schmidt Landschaftsarchitekten

↑↑ | Soccer field and skating area
↖ | Play area
↑ | Site plan

Central Park
Munich

In addition to the leisure functions for residents and play areas for children and adults, the park serves as a center for interaction and unwinding for the employees of the adjacent commercial districts. At the core of the park are the thematic gardens. They present abstractions of the landscapes located between Munich and the Alps. There is a rock garden, a pebble garden, a mountain lake with prism-like structures, a hilly landscape with spherical elements, a forest garden with Juneberry trees, and a field and meadow garden. All gardens offer exploration and play opportunities for children and adults. Each individual can select a play area to swing, slide, climb, play chess or discover nature. A sophisticated skating park is located between the thematic garden and the extensive lawns.

PROJECT FACTS **Address:** Parkstadt Schwabing, Munich, Germany. **Client:** City-Tech, Munich. **Completion:** 2002. **Materials:** stones and sand. **Theme:** landscape for playing.

↑ | Play areas
↓ | Mountain lake garden

↓ | View of park

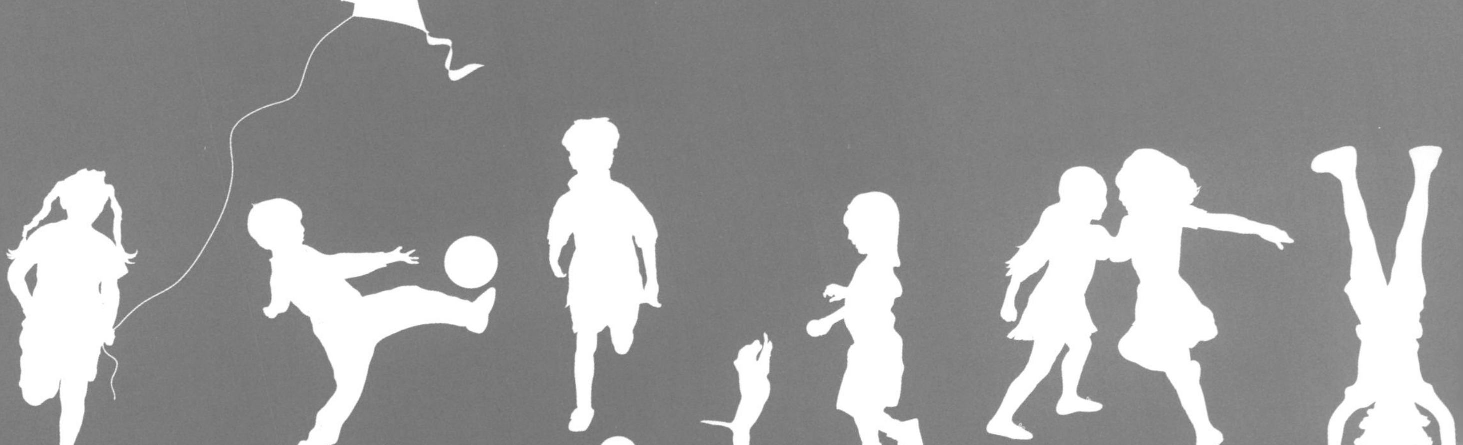

SPORTS

NATURE | Carve

↖↖ | **Black rubber landscape with playing elements**
↖ | **Trampoline integrated within the play landscape**
↑ | **View from one black rubber landscape to the other**

Potgieterstraat
Amsterdam

The inner "court" of the new Potgieterstraat consists of two black rubber landscapes with integrated playing elements flanked by box-shaped benches with a water play area at the center. The plan includes two wide sidewalks with the playing and seating area in between. The grid of trees was restored, reconnecting the street to the line of trees further down. Although residents favored a wide pedestrian and cycling area, politicians insisted on a bike-path on which scooter bikes and mopeds are also allowed. Playing kids are protected by a hedge. The realization of the new Potgieterstraat has been an extensive and long participative process resulting in many compromises. As a result, it created a firm base for the interaction of residents and has become one of the liveliest streets of the area.

PROJECT FACTS **Address:** Potgieterstraat, Amsterdam, The Netherlands. **Client:** the municipality of Amsterdam. **Completion:** 2010. **Materials:** EPDM rubber, metal and wood. **Theme:** ground landscape.

↑ | **Slide integrated within the black rubber landscape**
↓ | **A crawling tunnel perforates the landscape**

NATURE   CARVE

← | Play landscape located within a public courtyard
↓ | Rubber landscape provides resting possibilities and chalk drawing
→ | Playing pole
↘ | Site plan and elevation

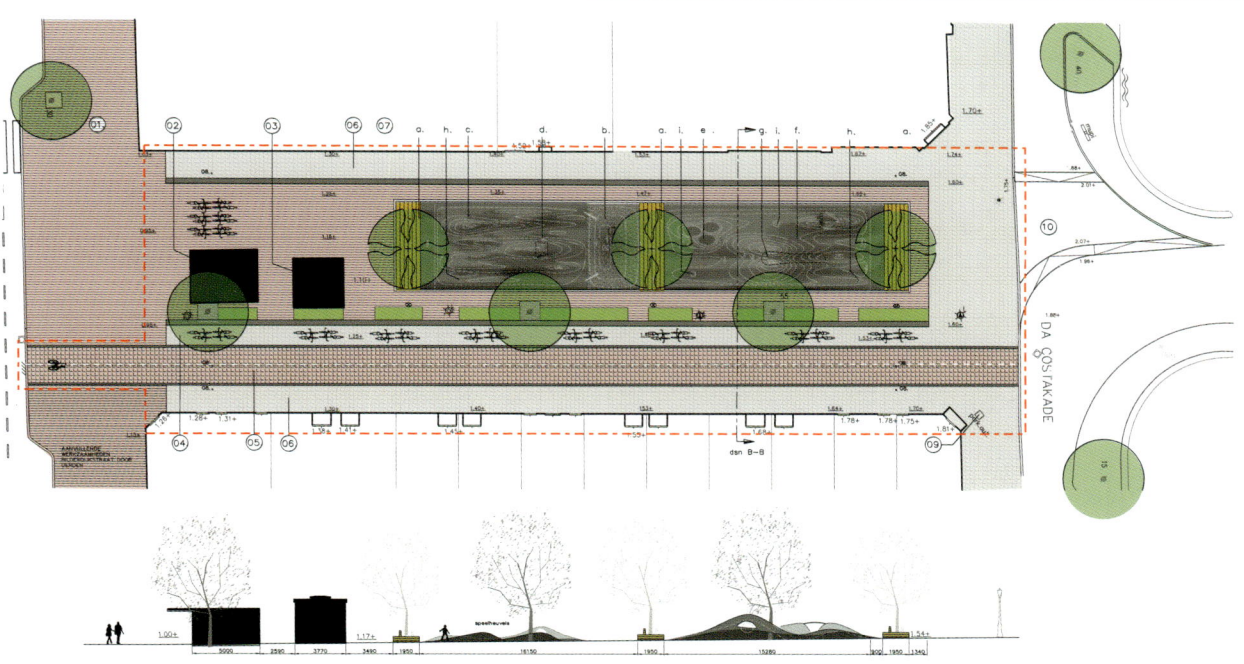

POTGIETERSTRAAT

SPORTS | 2012 Architecten

↑ | Play towers with hanging nets

Wikado Playground
Rotterdam

For the "Kinderparadijs Meidoorn" foundation, 2012 Architecten designed a new playground on their 1,200 square meter plot. The existing playground was in a bad shape and in need of renovation. 2012 Architecten mapped the old situation and selected the elements that were fit for re-use in a new playground. After this process a design was made. Five (discarded) rotor blades were used to create a maze like space with a panna court in the center, placed on the existing concrete circle. Four towers were placed around it, each with a distinctive character. Between the towers a net is hanging. This is functioning as a climbing structure, but will also prevent balls ending up in the garden of the neighbors.

PROJECT FACTS Location: Rotterdam, The Netherlands. **Completion:** 2008. **Materials:** windmill wings, rotor blades, metal, net, concrete and existing trees. **Theme:** super-use.

↑ | General view
↓ | Rotor blade with openings for interior and exterior play

↓ | Hanging net

SPORTS   2012 ARCHITECTEN

← | Bird's-eye view
↓ | Children play inside perforated rotor blade
→ | Tower equipped with a lower and a higher slide

WIKADO PLAYGROUND

SPORTS | Atelier Remy & Veenhuizen

↑ | Child standing on fence recession
↖ | Fence extends out as a platform for playing
↑ | Seating nook

Playground Fence
Dordrecht

The Playground Fence by Tejo Remy is a translation of what is normally a mundane object – by manipulating the fence with protrusions and recessions, seats, benches, nooks and play spaces for children were created. Instead of the initial concept of adding nothing to the schoolyard, an existing element was used and converted. Part of the fence was transformed into sitting spots for the students in order to create meeting places. The work covers five fence parts, replicates the measurements and color of the existing Heras fence.

PROJECT FACTS **Address:** Willem de Zwijgerlaan 2, 3314 NX Dordrecht, The Netherlands. **Client:** Primary School "Hetnoorderlicht", Dordrecht. **Completion:** 2005. **Materials:** steel, powder, coating. **Theme:** fence as a playground.

↑ | Children play in platform
↓ | Protrusions and recessions of the fence

SPORTS | Carve

↑ | Climbing frips and tactile elements

Van Campenvaart
The Hague

This new playground was created on an existing lawn and shaped like a folded red blanket with a strong graphical character. By constructing creases between ramps, several angles were created. The undefined possibilities of the field challenge the boundaries of both (partially) disabled and non-disabled children. Intersecting routes allow children with different abilities to meet and help each other. In the playing field, different climbing grips and tactile elements were added, as well as a moving rubber mat. Whisper tubes, a wide slide, a "concave" revolving disc and a hammock constitute additional play elements.

PROJECT FACTS **Address:** Van Campenvaart, The Hague, The Netherlands. **Client:** municipality of The Hague. **Completion:** 2010. **Materials:** wood, concrete, metal, ropes, hammock and rubber (flooring). **Theme:** landscape blanket.

↑ | View to Whisper tubes and concave revolving disc
↓ | Playground on existing lawn

SPORTS   CARVE

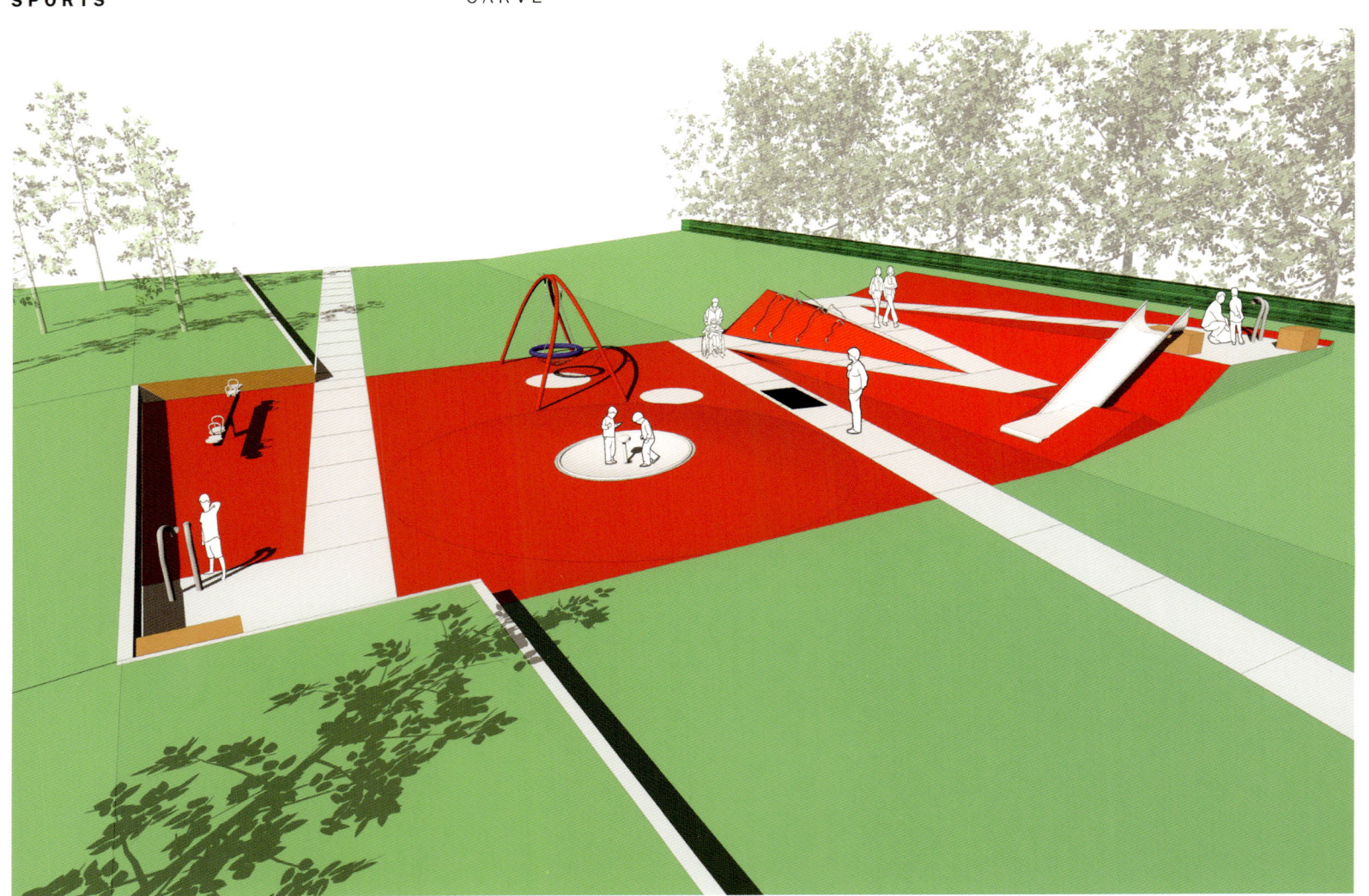

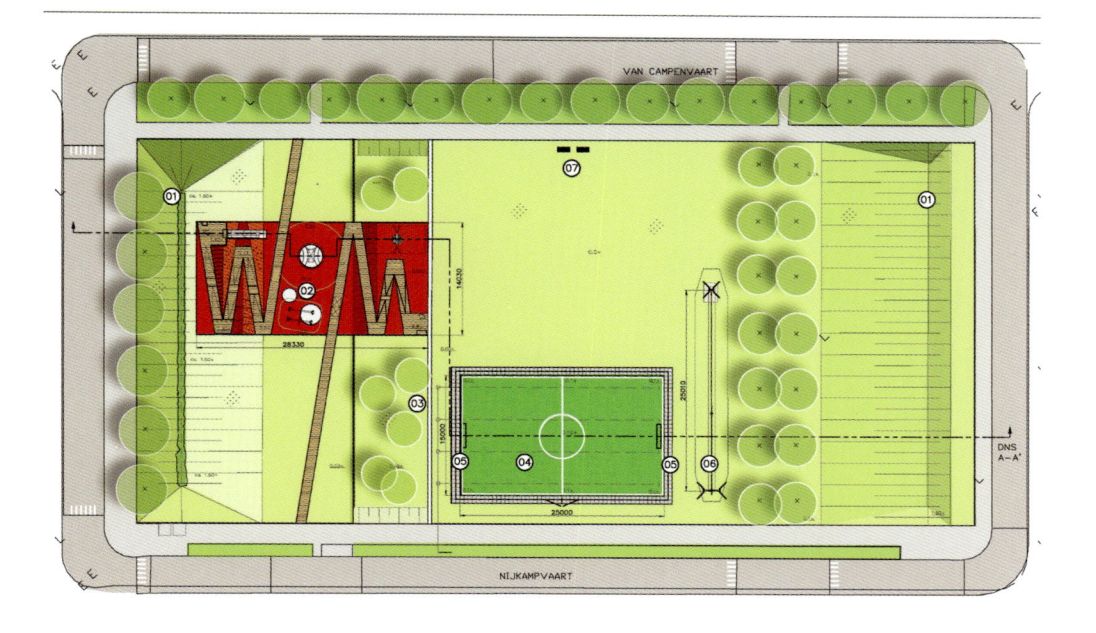

↖↖ | Axonometric view
←← | Creases in between ramps
↑ | Detail of climbing grips and tactile surfaces
← | Floor plan and elevation

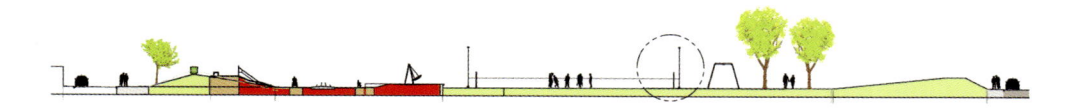

SPORTS | BASE

↑ | **Play structure**

Park des Prés de Lyon
La Chapelle St-Luc

Located in La Chapelle St-Luc, on the outskirts of Troyes, the "Prés de Lyon" was designed in the 1970s. When the park became run-down, the town council contracted landscape architects to make it more accessible and attractive. BASE renovated the ground, pathways, entrances and planted plots, proposing several play areas. A 700 square meter concrete skate park was built, along with children playgrounds, a miniature golf course, pétanque playing areas, and a health and fitness trail. At the center of the park, on a vast plain liable to flooding, BASE proposed building a 170 square meter solarium facing south for sunbathing and as a relaxation area. It is accessed by wooden pontoons and banks, located one-meter high, safe from potential flood risks. Integrated lighting is provided in the structure and pontoons.

| **PROJECT FACTS** | **Address:** Rue du Maréchal Leclerc, 10600 La Chapelle Saint Luc, France. **Client:** Communauté d'agglomération troyenne Ville de La Chappelle St-Luc. **Other creatives:** AAVP architect / ON / Cabinet Merlin BET. **Completion:** 2006. **Materials:** wood and concrete. **Theme:** landscape for playing.

↑ | **Sunbathing and relaxation area**
↓ | **Wooden pontoons lead to sunbathing area**

SPORTS BASE

↑ | **General view**
← | **Site plan**

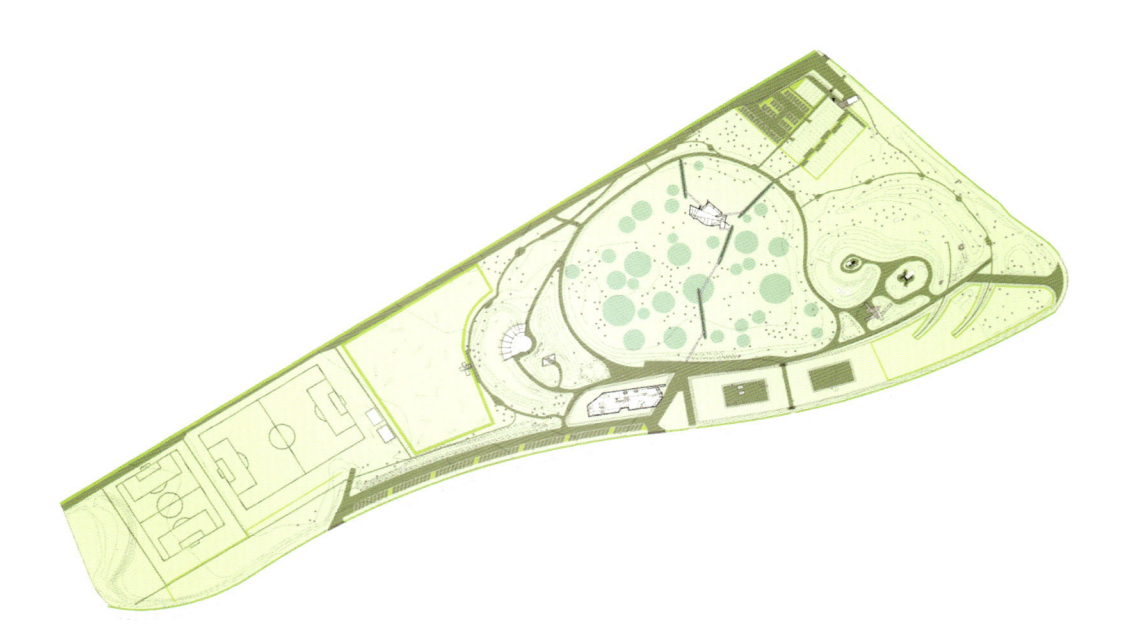

PARK DES PRÉS DE LYON

← | Skating slopes
↓ | Concrete skate park

SPORTS | EARTHSCAPE

↑ | White coral for playing and resting

Urban Dock LaLaport Toyosu
Tokyo

The theme of this project is ocean and voyagers. Three waves of "green," "water," and "earth" were layered over the reclaimed land of a former shipyard, with a cafe, radio station, and museum resembling several "islands," and white benches with foam and coral motifs floating above the waves. The Wave Garden depicts waves topped with white benches in the shape of foam and coral. The undulating ground is very popular with children, and even though there is no play equipment, the space invites people to spontaneously run around and play. LaLaport Toyosu incorporates unique and playful design concepts, such as designs based on the memories of the old shipyard; areas for appreciating the beautiful sunsets on the ocean horizon in the evening, and various others landscape graphics elements.

PROJECT FACTS **Address:** 2-4-9 Toyosu Koto-ku Tokyo, Japan. **Client:** Mitsui Fudosan Co. Ltd., Ishikawajima-Harima Heavy. **Architect:** Laguarda Low Architects. **Completion:** 2006. **Materials:** soil cement, tiles (white lines), FRP (bench). **Theme:** wave and floating.

↑ | Children running at the memorial dock
↓ | Bird's-eye view of Wave Garden

SPORTS EARTHSCAPE

URBAN DOCK LALAPORT TOYOSU

↖↖ | Wave Garden raises its surfaces to become slides
←← | Slides in Wave Garden
↑ | Site plan
← | Fountain pop-up jets

SPORTS | Bekkering Adams Architecten

↑ | Top view of "secret garden" and sports area

Public Playground Rotterdam
Rotterdam

Located on the Mullerpier in Rotterdam, the site serves a schoolyard for the primary school nearby and a public square for its vicinity, which includes a home for the elderly, a business center, a theater and housing. The proposal for the playground was set up in cooperation with the school, parents, and neighbors. The demands were more green, shelter and better play areas. The final plan includes a sports area where older children can play competitive games and a smaller square where younger children can play in a diverse way. Around the square is a green hedge, which together with the green rubber underground reflects the theme of "a secret garden". The resulting site challenges children to play in diverse ways, while adults use the square as an outdoor facility of their neighborhood.

PROJECT FACTS **Address:** Mullerkade 173, 3024 EH Rotterdam, The Netherlands. **Client:** Municipality of Rotterdam. **Completion:** 2007. **Materials:** concrete, rubber (flooring) and metal. **Theme:** secret garden.

↑ | "Secret garden" play area
↓ | Children ride their bikes following the colorful paths

↓ | Children slide in "secret garden" play element

SPORTS   BEKKERING ADAMS ARCHITECTEN

↑ | Site plan
← | Sports courtyard

PUBLIC PLAYGROUND ROTTERDAM

↑ | Bird's-eye view
← | Wooden bench for resting or eating

SPORTS

Carve, in collaboration with
Marie-Laure Hoedemakers

↑↑ | **King-crawl, sliding tubes**
↖ | **Skating landscape**
↑ | **Detail skating surface**

Bijlmerpark
Amsterdam

Bijlmerpark consists of a park around a central sports facility with residential units along its flanks. The new housing faces the park and the sports park is within walking distance of the residents. This area in the center of the park is linked to the main circular pedestrian and bicycle routes. It contains a ball court, a playing strip, the "king crawler", a skate park, and a water and sand playground. The playing strip contains yellow frames on a pink safety surfacing, with different rope bridges and a zip line connected to the "king crawler", a multilevel playing wall that incorporates facilities for the manager and public toilets. A skate park is hidden on top of a hill and the top of another contains a landscape for young children with sandboxes and water jets.

PROJECT FACTS **Address:** Bijlmerpark, Bijlmer-Centrum, Amsterdam, The Netherlands. **Client:** the municipality of Amsterdam, Stadsdeel Zuidoost. **Completion:** 2011. **Materials:** plastic, metal, rubber, metal mesh. **Theme:** sport and game esplanade.

↑ | **King-crawl, children climbing and crawling inside**
↓ | **Detail of mesh surface**

↓ | **View inside the king-crawl play area**

SPORTS   CARVE

← | Detail of metal sliding tubes
↓ | Site plan

↑ | Yellow climbing parcour
← | Sports and games esplanade

SPORTS | EARTHSCAPE

↑ | **Kids mountain**

Lazona Kawasaki Plaza
Kanagawa

The area around Kawasaki Station used to be a dark industrial zone. The designers revamped the area and involved the local people in various "stages" such as playgrounds for children, places for mothers with little children, event stages, etc. The area in front of the Lazona facility will be the station's new west exit and the entrance to the city for visitors. To add cheer to it, the natural landscape was turned into play equipment. The kids' mountain play area involves climbing holds on a hill of three-sided polygons. At the Amidakuji (ghost leg) area, words are inscribed into the path using Hiragana words for nature and English words for cities and society. The result is a game in which words connect, creating a new vocabulary about nature and cities.

PROJECT FACTS

Address: 72-1 Horikawa-cho Saiwai-ku Kawasaki city Kanagawa 212-0013, Japan. **Client:** Toshiba, Mitsui Fudosan Group. **Architect:** Ricardo Bofill Leví + Yamashita Sekkei. **Completion:** 2006. **Materials:** rubber, concrete, artificial turf, climbing holds (kids' mountain) / stone, stainless steel and brass. **Theme:** kids mountain, discovery.

↑ | Play mountain aerial view
↓ | Children climbing play mountain

↓ | Three-sided polygons form a play mountain

SPORTS   EARTHSCAPE

← | Bird's-eye view of words' path
↓ | Children sliding at play mountain

LAZONA KAWASAKI PLAZA

← | Children chasing the words' path
↓ | Detail of play mountain

SPORTS | KuKuk

↑ | Slide tower with small slide for disabled children

KuKuk Playground
Zurich

An adventure trail crosses the schoolyard – children pass through a field of columns, a climbing structure and graduated pedestals to reach a tower with a handicap-compatible slide. The structure made of poles and ropes also allows wheelchair users to pull themselves through. The wall maze provides many sensory perceptions. Colorful play objects and a rubber granulate floor suitable for wheelchairs provide design accents and facilitate orientation. The landscape architecture office of Berchtold Lenzin of Zurich was responsible for the overall design. KuKuk (Kunst Kultur Konzeption) of Stuttgart, Germany conceived and implemented the handicap-accessible play and adventure space.

PROJECT FACTS **Address:** Mutschellenstrasse 102, 8038 Zurich, Switzerland. **Client:** Green city of Zurich, Thomas Bachofner. **Completion:** 2011. **Materials:** black locust wood, ropes, plexiglass and stainless steel. **Theme:** handicap-accessible play and adventure space.

↑ | Slightly tilted timber wall maze with plexiglass windows and a funhouse a distorting mirror
↓ | Wall maze with wooden platforms and hammocks

SPORTS   KUKUK

← | Palisades bridge and rope for balancing
↓ | Rope forest with loops and vines suitable for wheelchair users
→ | Big sliding tower
↘ | Wall maze sketch

KUKUK PLAYGROUND

SPORTS | Martha Schwartz Partners

↑ | Bird's nest swing, swings above blobs

St Mary's Churchyard
London

The key design goals for St Mary's Churchyard were to reorganize the park while retaining its positive historic qualities, link the park to the city, incorporate healthy existing trees into the design, and ultimately to make the park a safe, accessible and desirable place for the community. These goals should be achieved by incorporating park access, safety and activity into the design. During the works to landscape the churchyard, workmen came across a number of old vaults and burial plots. These were carefully recorded by an archaeologist and left undisturbed. Today the site remains a consecrated ground and continues to be an open space for the use and enjoyment of children and the greater public.

PROJECT FACTS **Address:** Newington Butts, London, United Kingdom. **Client:** London Borough of Southwark. **Completion:** 2008. **Materials:** rubber, metal, ropes and plastic. **Theme:** blobs.

↑ | **General view**
↓ | **Spring "disc" toy**

↓ | **Orange climbing blobs**

SPORTS   MARTHA SCHWARTZ PARTNERS

↑ | Detail of rubber ground surface
← | Climbing blobs

ST MARY'S CHURCHYARD

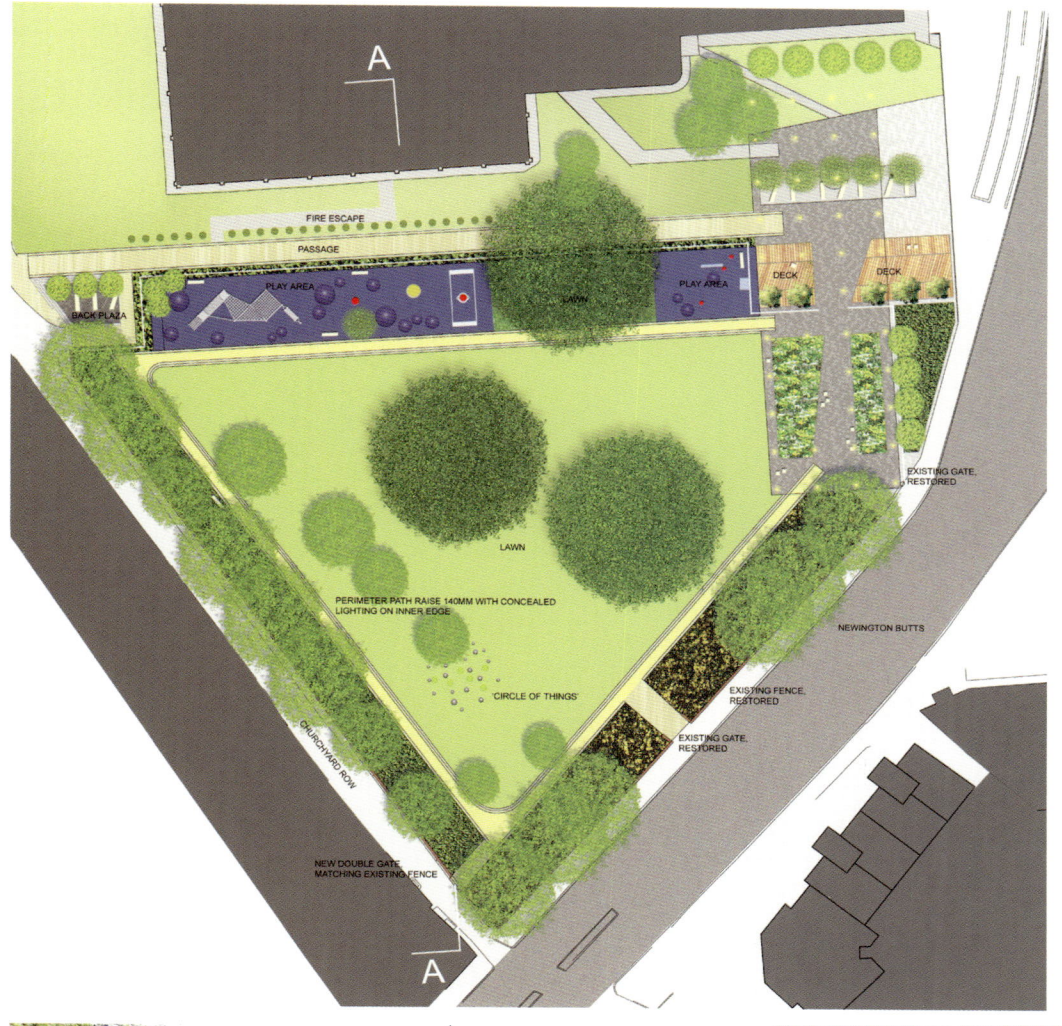

← | Site plan
↓ | Parkspace with black and white spheres sprouting up like mushrooms

SPORTS | Carve

↑ | Swings at different heights

Van Beuningenplein
Amsterdam

Parked cars dominated the public space both physically and functionally. Thus, the city of Amsterdam decided to construct an underground parking garage with a new play and sports area on top. In the former situation the "van Beuningenplein" was hidden from view by cars, fencing, and poorly maintained green. Eliminating these obstructions connected the surrounding houses to the square, integrating it once again into the neighborhood. The intense color of the lounge area, skate area and sport court gives the park a unique and recognizable identity. Along the façades hedges were placed in strategic locations leaving space for local initiatives, like a bench or a façade garden. The boundary between private and public has become less rigid, resulting in a colorful and lively setting.

PROJECT FACTS **Address:** Amsterdam, The Netherlands. **Client:** City of Amsterdam. **Landscape architects:** Dijk&Co Landscape architecture. **Completion:** 2011. **Materials:** wood, metal mesh, ropes and rubber. **Theme:** sport field, water feature and ice skating (winter time).

↑ | General view
↓ | Swings with water feature

↓ | Rope web to climb up and down the tower

SPORTS   CARVE

VAN BEUNINGENPLEIN

↖↖ | View of playground from surrounding garden
←← | Skateboard area
↑ | Children climbing up the slide
← | Pavilion

SPORTS | selgascano

↑ | Curvaceous skate park

Merida Factory Youth Movement
Merida

Merida Factory Youth Movement is an example of the cooperation of the regional government, the community, and local designers to meet the needs of youth of the back streets of Spanish cities. It was designed using recycled furniture, inexpensive building materials and temporary solutions. It provides the youth with a place to skateboard, dance hip-hop, climb rocks, create graffiti – whatever they would otherwise do in much more sinister surroundings. There is also a computer lab and a dance studio, both 800 square meters in size. Meeting rooms and spaces for theater, video and music are also included. This is one of several "youth factories": recreational centers and places that are inclusive, open and safe.

PROJECT FACTS **Address:** Calle Mirandilla, 06800 Mérida, Spain. **Client:** ISPT. **Completion:** 2011. **Materials:** polycarbonate and concrete. **Theme:** skate and climbing park.

↑ | Canopies protect from rain and sun
↓ | Biking within the plastic "cloud"

SPORTS   SELGASCANO

MERIDA FACTORY YOUTH MOVEMENT

←← | Organically shaped canopy
↑ | Floor plan
← | Polycarbonate red canopy supported by programmatic pillars

SPORTS | SO-IL

↑ | **Aerial view**

Pole Dance
New York

SO-IL designed a participatory environment that reframes the conceptual relation between humankind and structure. It consists of an interconnected system of poles and nets whose equilibrium is constantly affected by human action and environmental factors, such as rain and wind. The small courtyard adjacent to the main space holds an immersive, interactive portion where visitors can create and control a rich sound experience from within the installation. Eight poles contain "accelerometers" – electronic devices that measure the motion of the poles – connected to custom software that converts motion into tones specifically composed for the installation. An iPhone application allows visitors to affect the quality of sound for each pole in real time. By turning the effects levels up or down the audience can collaboratively vote to change the active sound of their environment. The application also collects the movements of the interactive poles and visualizes the dynamic activity and movement within the installation in real time.

PROJECT FACTS **Address:** MoMA PS1 22-25 Jackson Avenue, Long Island City, NY 11101, USA. **Client:** MoM /MoMA PS1. **Structural engineer:** Buro Happold. **Interactive sound installation:** Arup Acoustics. **Graphics/identity:** 2x4. **Completion:** 2010. **Materials:** fiberglass poles, nylon net, windsurf mast base, plastic balls and accelerometers. **Theme:** interactive environment, multimedia installation.

↑ | Open net covers the entire field and controls pivot of the poles
↓ | Bird's eye view of building site

↓ | Top view, pool

SPORTS SO-IL

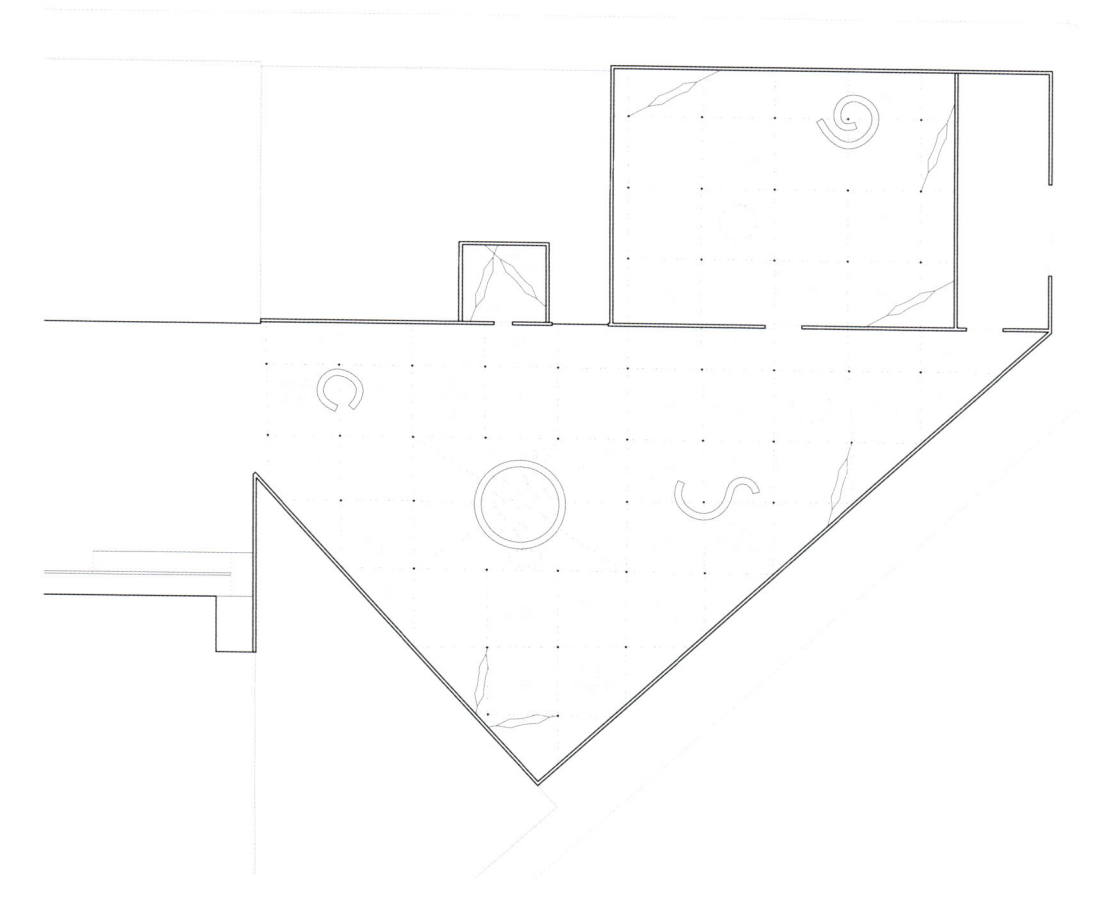

POLE DANCE

219

←← | Interconnected system of poles and nets
↙↙ | Pole dance diagram
← | Floor plan
↓ | Nine meter high poles connected by bungee cords

SPORTS

Van Rooijen Nourbakhsh
Architecten

↑ | New building entrance

Playground Building
Utrecht

In an inner courtyard close to the city center of Utrecht a playground serves the children of the neighborhood. The old building on the playground was replaced by a modest, durable and safe new building that upgraded the playground and appealed to children. Within a very tight budget a colorful light-hearted element was designed and installed at the playground. The building has a separate section for a kindergarten. A movable partition allows its spaces to be interlinked to serve different activities and multiple uses. The relationship between inside and outside is playfully strengthened by specific openings and windows. A large covered canopy for sheltered play adorns the front of the building. Natural wood and colors determine the cozy and comfortable atmosphere of the interior.

PROJECT FACTS **Address:** Bloesemstraat 25A, 3581 Utrecht, The Netherlands. **Client:** Municipality of Utrecht. **Completion:** 2010. **Materials:** wood, glass. **Theme:** playful sculptural building.

↑ | Interior view kindergarten area
↓ | Front view

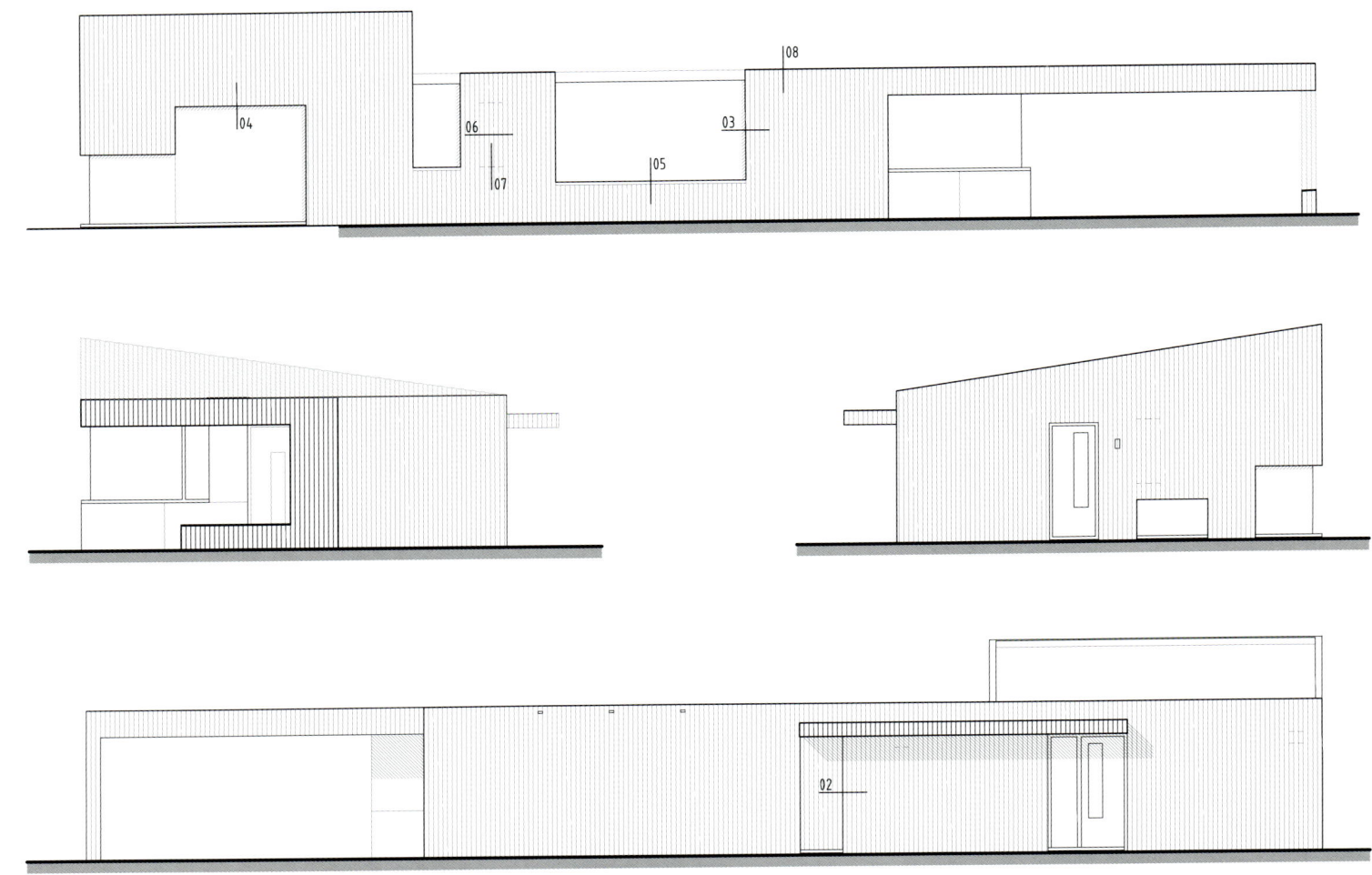

↑ | Elevations
← | Interior-exterior play areas are connected by large window openings

PLAYGROUND BUILDING

↑ | Wooden surfaces in building interior
← | Building's floor plan

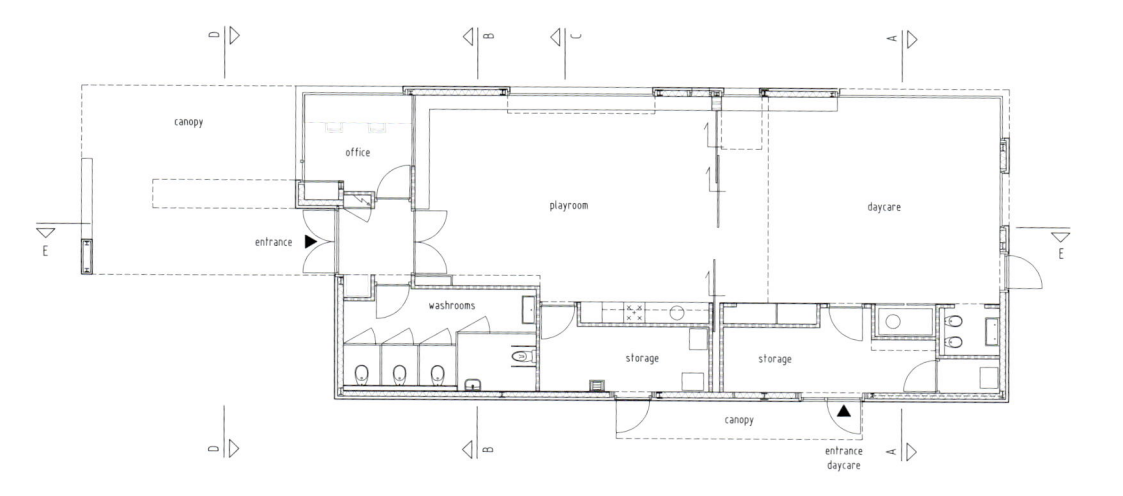

SPORTS | Carve

↑ | **Boulderwall**

Wall-Holla
Amsterdam

The city council of Purmerend invited Carve to design a new schoolyard. The requirements included a football field, a climbing facility and playground equipment accommodating over 60 children. As a result the Wall-Holla was created. This vertical urban play-structure combines several functions that appeal to different age groups. It is a crawl-through maze, a climbing wall and a lounge object. Its modular system allows it to be made in different sizes and various combinations. It can be equipped with a football goal, slides or fireman poles. The undulating ribbons create a vertical, ever changing maze, appealing to children's fantasy. The surface varies between soft EPDM, rope mesh and open grid, encouraging children to sit, walk, hang, swing, slide, run, jump, vault and hide.

PROJECT FACTS **Address:** Amsterdam, The Netherlands. **Client:** district Zuid of Amsterdam. **Completion:** 2008. **Materials:** steel, wire mesh / polyferro cables, epoxy-raisin climbing holds and EPDM rubber. **Theme:** vertical urban play structure.

↑ | **Kid climbing through maze structure**
↓ | **Detail of different undulating ribbons**

↓ | **Undulated ribbon with an opening**

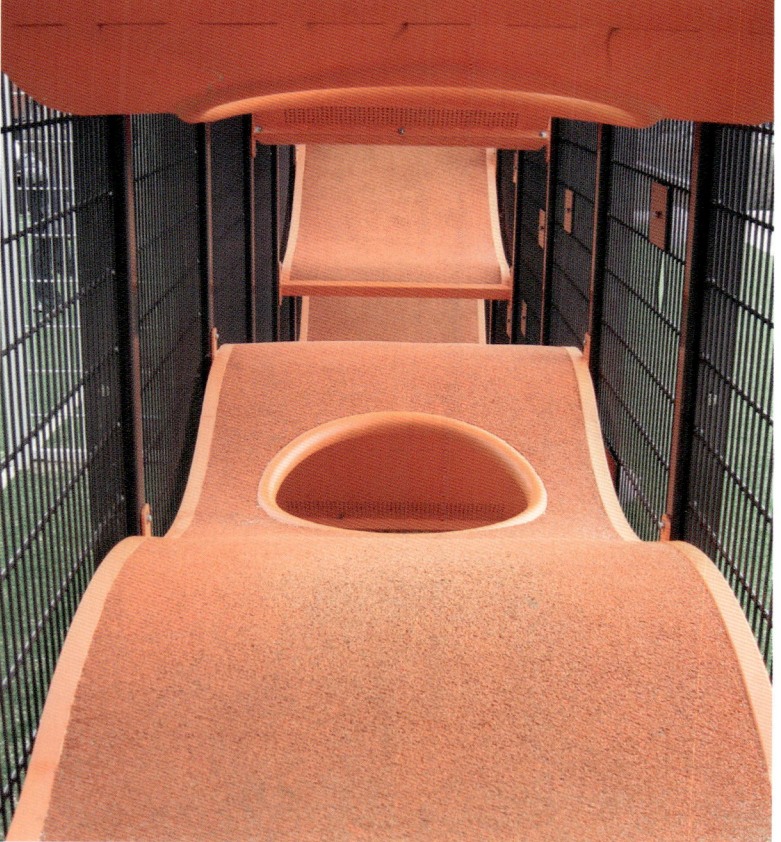

SPORTS   CARVE

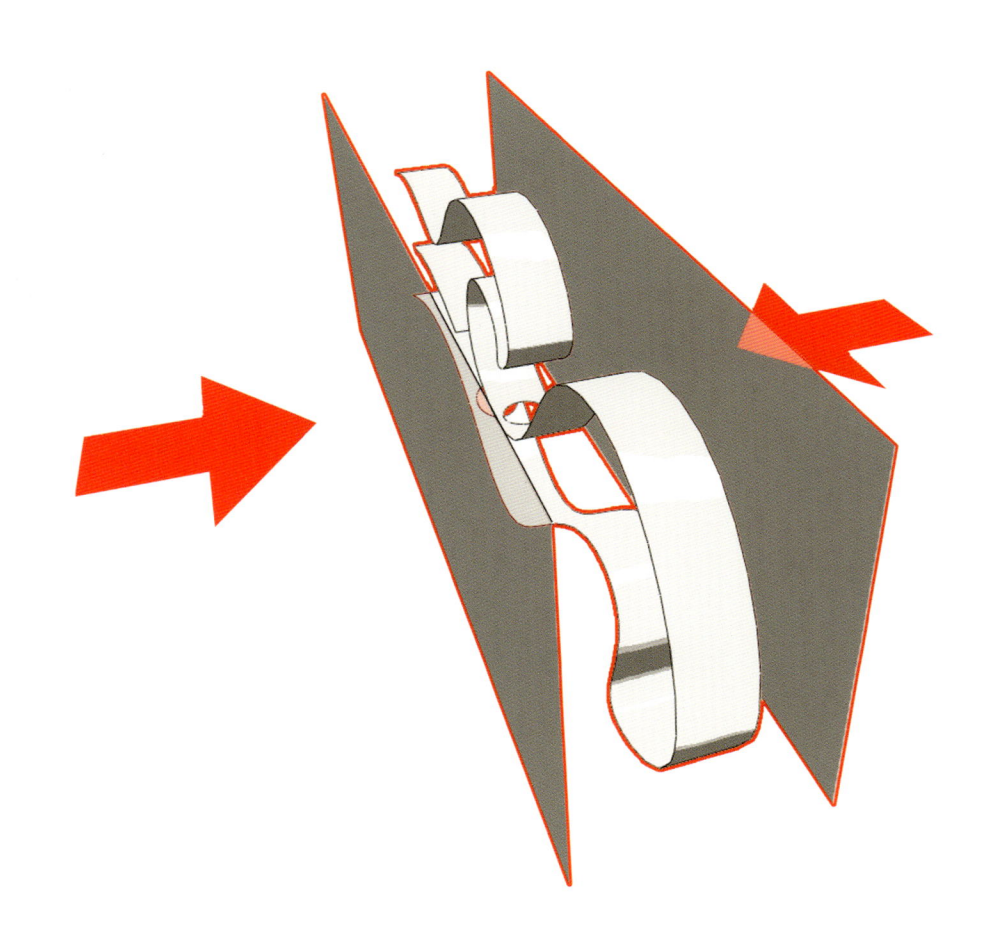

← | Diagrammatic drawing
↓ | Vertical playstructure

WALL-HOLLA

↑ | Wire mesh surface with opening to enter and exit structure
← | Conceptual drawing

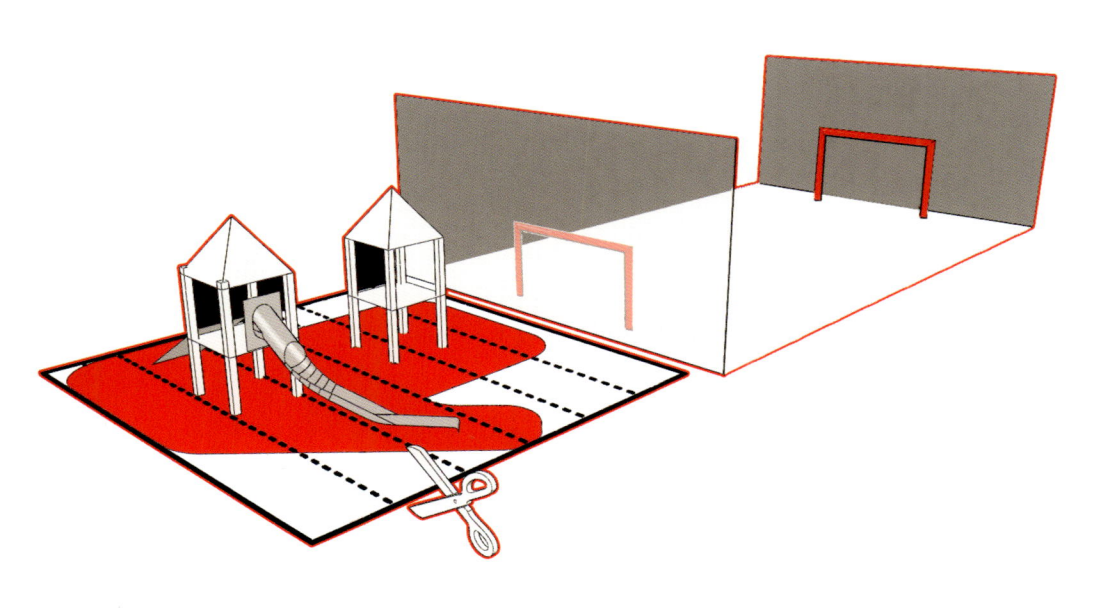

SPORTS | Basurama

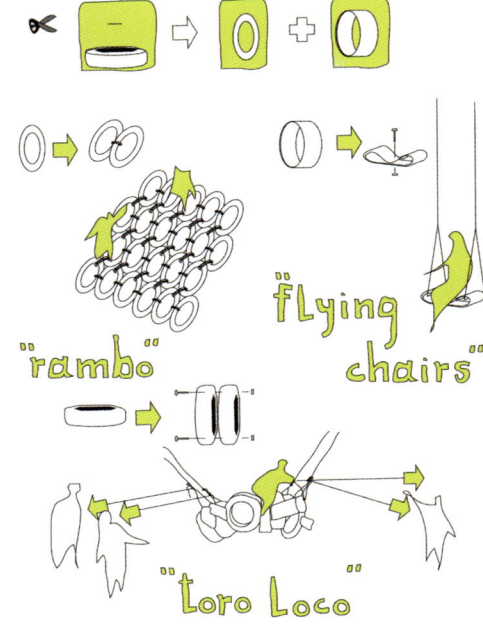

↙↙ | "Rambo" climbing tire wall
↑↑ | Design diagram
↑ | Flying chairs

RUS Lima, Public Amusement Autopark

Lima

Following the basic structure of the draft RUS (Urban Solid Waste) invited the community and various local artists to activate the space by proposing a number of attractions and games, and other interventions of collective imagination; the rail infrastructure became a celebration of public space and reflection: a small amusement park. It is equipped with swings, climbers, and ziplines, mostly made from old tires. This playground uses recycled materials, such as, car parts and tires as a form of a paradoxical reflection about public and private transport.

PROJECT FACTS **Address:** Avenida Primavera / Avenida Aviación, Surquillo district, Lima, Peru. **Client:** Spanish Development Agency. **Collaborators:** Christians Luna, Sandra Nakamura, Camila Bustamante, Recurseo, Playstationvagon y El Codo. **Completion:** 2010. **Materials:** tires and ropes. **Theme:** re-use of abandoned infrastructure as a playground.

↑ | "Crazy bull"
↓ | Public Amusement Autopark

SPORTS

Navadijos Tarsoly
Arquitectos

↑ | **Ball game**

Umbraculum and Children's Games Garden
Boadilla del Monte, Madrid

This project solves the integration of a tilted field of 1,072 square meters, including the renovation of the existing play area. Navadijos Tarsoly Arquitectos designed a large game room, airy and cool, which also integrates the existing pavilion. The structure, with no diagonals, disappears between two sheets of polycarbonate, thereby creating a smooth and translucent membrane. To facilitate visual control, visibility extends to the maximum horizontal area of the courtyard, where play areas are defined by a fence-abacus, inviting children to play together without perceived barriers. A landscape of small rubber hills and miscellaneous playground items created especially for the completed project provides space for recreation.

PROJECT FACTS **Address:** Calle Monte Romanillos, Boadilla del Monte, Madrid, Spain. **Client:** Ciudad Infantil Mirabal S.L. **Landscape architects:** GHB Landscape Architects. **Completion:** 2008. **Materials:** steel, polycarbonate sheets, rubber floor and sand. **Theme:** all weather playground.

↑ | Sand pit and tricycle area
↓ | Sand pit play area

SPORTS NAVADIJOS TARSOLY ARQUITECTOS

← | Ondulated landscape
↓ | Floor plan
→ | Covered play area
↘ | Ball game

UMBRACULUM AND CHILDREN'S GAMES GARDEN

Index
Arch.

tects' Index

ARCHITECTS' INDEX

2012 Architecten

Ermandtspad 5
3061 CE, Rotterdam (The Netherlands)
T +31.10.4664444
info@2012architecten.nl
www.2012architecten.nl

→ 170

24° Studio

5-2-21 Sakaguchi Dori
Chuo-ku, Kobe 651-0062 (Japan)
T +81.78.2426611
info@24d-studio.com
www.24d-studio.com

→ 78

AMMA architecture de paysage

Architecte paysagiste agréé AAPQ/AAPC
3 Napoléon-Beaumont
Sainte-Catherine-la-Jacques-Cartier,
Quebec G3N 0N9 (Canada)
T +1.418.8754014
info@ammaarchitecturedepaysage.com
www.ammaarchitecturedepaysage.com

→ 86

ANNABAU Architektur und Landschaft

Choriner Straße 55
10435 Berlin (Germany)
T +49.30.33021585
F +49.30.33021586
mail@annabau.com
www.annabau.com

→ 96

Aspect Studios

Studio 61 – Level 6
61 Marlborough St
Surry Hills, 2010 NSW (Australia)
T +61.2.96997182
F +61.2.96997192
aspectsydney@aspect.net.au
www.aspect.net.au

→ 100

BASE

259, rue Saint-Martin
75003 Paris (France)
T +33.1.42778181
F +33.1.42778198
paris@baseland.fr
www.baseland.fr

→ 56, 180

Basurama

Avenida Daroca n°49, callejón
28017 Madrid (Spain)
info@basurama.org
www.basurama.org

→ 228

Bekkering Adams Architecten

Pelgrimsstraat 1
3029 BH Rotterdam (The Netherlands)
T +31.10.4258166
info@bekkeringadams.nl
www.bekkeringadams.nl

→ 188

birke · zimmermann landschaftsarchitekten

Wichertstraße 5
10439 Berlin (Germany)
T +49.30.484 4019
info@birkezimmermann.de
www.birkezimmermann.de

→ 24

Carve

Kortenaerplein 34
1057 Amsterdam (The Netherlands)
T +31.20.4275711
F +31.20.4275712
info@carve.nl
www.carve.nl

→ 82, 126, 166, 176, 192, 208, 224

CPG Australia

469 La Trobe Street
3205 Melbourne, VIC (Australia)
T +61.3.99937888
F +61.3.99937999
melbourne@au.cpg-global.com
www.cpg-global.com

→ 104

E.F.E.U. Riederer und Münch

Lottumstraße 10A
10119 Berlin (Germany)

→ 64

EARTHSCAPE

2-14-6 Ebisu Shibuya-ku
Tokyo 150-0013 (Japan)
T +81.3.62773970
F +81.3.34733970
info@earthscape.co.jp
www.earthscape.co.jp

→ 184, 196

Erect Architecture

22b Regent Studios
8 Andrews Road
London E8 4QN (United Kingdom)
T +44.20.70332779
F +44.20.80825838
mail@erectarchitecture.uk
www.erectarchitecture.co.uk

→ 108

geskes.hack landscape architects

Keplerstraße 4
10589 Berlin (Germany)
T +49.30.76239740
mail@geskes-hack.de
www.geskes-hack.de

→ 90, 112

Jane Hutton & Adrian Blackwell

17 Paton Road
Toronto, ON M6H 1R7 (Canada)
416 709-1471
jhutton@gsd.harvard.edu

→ 120

Jeavons Landscape Architects

1st Floor, 717 Nicholson Street
Carlton North VIC 3054 (Autralia)
www.jeavons.com.au

→ 130

KuKuk

Rosenwiesstraße 17
70567 Stuttgart (Germany)
T +49.711.3421550
F +49.711.34215520
spielraum@zumKuKuk.de
www.zumkukuk.de

→ 200

Kunder³ Landschaftsarchitektur

Grundstraße 5
70771 Leinfelden-Echterdingen (Germany)
T +49.711.526014
F +49.711.5504508
www.kunder-landschaftsarchitektur.de

→ 94

LAND-I archicolture

Via Madonna dei Monti n.50
00184 Rome (Italy)
archicolture@gmail.com
www.archicolture.com

→ 134

Martha Schwartz Partners

65–69 East Road
London N1 6AH (United Kingdom)
T +44.20.75497497
F +44.20.72500988
mail@marthaschwartz.com
www.marthaschwartz.com

→ 136, 204

Monstrum

Avedøreholmen 84
2650 Hvidovre (Denmark)
T +45.33.221077
mail@monstrum.dk
monstrum.dk

→ 16, 28, 36, 44, 52, 68

Mulders vandenBerk Architecten

Leliëndaalstraat 12
1013 BP Amsterdam (The Netherlands)
T +31.20.7892696
info@muldersvandenberk.nl
www.muldersvandenberk.nl

→ 32

Navadijos Tarsoly Arquitectos

Calle Rios Rosas, 11, 6° Oficina
28013 Madrid (Spain)
T +34.91.4427674
arquitectos@navadijos-tarsoly.com
www.navadijos-tarsoly.com

→ 230

ARCHITECTS' INDEX

plancontext landschaftsarchitektur

Greifenhagener Straße 39
10437 Berlin (Germany)
T +49.30.44718831
F +49.30.44718832
info@plancontext.de
www.plancontext.de

→ **116, 140**

pro garten landschaftsarchitektur

Langenscheidtstraße 3
10827 Berlin (Germany)
T +49.30.21458991
F +49.30.21458992
buero@progarten-berlin.de
www.progarten-berlin.de

→ **12, 40**

Rainer Schmidt Landschaftsarchitekten

Klenzestraße 57c
80469 Munich (Germany)
T +49.89.2025350
F +49.89.20253530
info@rainerschmidt.com
www.schmidt-landschaftsarchitekten.de

→ **124, 144, 162**

Tejo Remy & Rene Veenhuizen

Uraniumweg 17
3542 AK Utrecht (The Netherlands)
T +31.30.2944945
atelier@remyveenhuizen.nl
www.remyveenhuizen.nl

→ **174**

RS+

Nałkowskiej 4a/49
43-100 Tychy (Poland)
T +48.605.636683
rsplus@rsplus.pl
www.rsplus.pl

→ **148**

selgascano

Guecho 27-SC
28023 Madrid (Spain)
T +34.913076481
selgascano1@gmail.com
www.selgascano.net

→ **212**

SO-IL

68 Jay Street, #501
11201 Brooklyn, New York (USA)
T+ 718.6246666
office@so-il.org
www.so-il.org

→ **216**

Space2place

The Mercantile Building
Suite 309 - 318 Homer Street
Vancouver, BC
V6B 2V2 (Canada)
T +1.604.646.4110
studio@space2place.com
www.space2place.com

→ **152**

Stoss Landscape Urbanism

423 West Broadway 304
02127 Boston. MA (USA)
T +1.617.4641142
F +1.617.4641142
www.stoss.net

→ **156**

Van Rooijen Nourbakhsh Architecten

Morgenstond 24
3454 ST De Meern (The Netherlands)
T + 31.30.6661368
F +31.30.6622174
vr.archi@inter.nl.net
www.vanrooijenarchitecten.nl

→ **220**

ver.de landschaftsarchitektur

Rindermarkt 2
85354 Freising (Germany)
T+49.8161.140993
F +49.8161.140996
info@gruppe-ver.de
www.gruppe-ver.de

→ **158**

PHOTO CREDITS

Zimmer.Obst GmbH
playground design

Am Winkel 9
15528 Spreenhagen (Germany)
T +49.336.3369890
F +49.336.33698929
spielraum@zimmerobst.de
www.zimmerobst.de

→ **20, 48, 60, 72**

24° Studio	78–81	Nielsen, Ole	16–19, 28–31, 36–39, 44–47, 52–55, 68–71
Allard van der Hoek	220–223		
Allen, Lewis	109 b., 110 a.	pro garten landschaftsarchitektur	12–15, 41–43
ANNABAU Architektur und Landschaft	96–99	Rainer Schmidt	
Asanuma, Shigeki, Koji Okumura/Forward Stroke	184–187, 196–199	Landschaftsarchitekten	124–127, 145 b.r., 163 a.
		Richter Spielgeräte	90, 91 a.l.r., 93
Backaert, Roel	33a., 34	Runge, Sebastian	40
Baronet, Robert, Jardins de Métis/ Reford Gardens	120–123	Schöpke, Jörn	60–63
		Sirtoli, Raffaella	162, 163 b.l.r.
BASE	56–59, 180–183	Space2place	152–155
basurama.org CC BY-NC-SA 3.0	228–229	© srnicholl – Fotolia.com	10, 76, 164
Bauer, Martin (portrait)	16	Stoss Landscape Urbanism	156, 157 b.l.r.
birke zimmermann Landschaftsarchitekten	24–27	Ta-Me, Hamish	101 b.r.
Carve	82–85, 126–129, 166–169, 176–179, 192–195, 208–211, 224–227	Tanguay, Louise	157 a.
		Tanguay, Louise, Jardins de Métis/ Redford Gardens	86–89
CPG Australia	104–107		
de Guzman, Miguel	230–233	Tejo Remy & Rene Veenhuizen	174–175
Digidaan (DD)	188–191	van der Hoek, Allard	170–173
Galindo, Michelle	64–67	van der Sar, Wouter	35 b.l.
Grandorge, David	108, 109 a., 110 b., 111	ver.de Landschaftsarchitektur	158–161
Groehn, Florian	100, 101 a.b.l., 102, 103	Weber, Thomas/KuKuk	200–203
Halbe, Roland/Artur Images	212–215	Zakrzewski, Tomasz	148–151
Hanenberg, Wim	32, 33 b.r., 35 a.	Zimmer/Obst	20–23, 72–75
Iwan Baan	216–219		
Jaekel, Martina	48–51	All other pictures, especially portraits and plans, were made available by the architects and designers.	
Joosten, Hanns	91 b., 92, 112–115		
Kunder Landschaftsarchitektur	94–95		
LAND-I archicolture	134–135		
Lichtschwärmer	116–119, 140–143		
Lloyd, Andrew	130–133	Cover front: Michelle Galindo	
Martha Schwartz Partners	136–139, 204–207	Cover back left: Roland Halbe/Artur Images	
Müller-Naumann, Stefan	144, 145 a.b.l., 146, 147	right: Jörn Schöpke	

IMPRINT

The Deutsche Nationalbibliothek lists this publication in the Deutsche Nationalbibliografie; detailed bibliographic data are available in the Internet at http://dnb.dnb.de

ISBN 978-3-03768-109-1

© 2012 by Braun Publishing AG
www.braun-publishing.ch

The work is copyright protected. Any use outside of the close boundaries of the copyright law, which has not been granted permission by the publisher, is unauthorized and liable for prosecution. This especially applies to duplications, translations, microfilming, and any saving or processing in electronic systems.

1st edition 2012

Selection of projects and layout: Michelle Galindo
English text editing: Cosima Talhouni
Graphic concept: ON Grafik | Tom Wibberenz
Reproduction: Bild1Druck GmbH, Berlin

All of the information in this volume has been compiled to the best of the editor's knowledge. It is based on the information provided to the publisher by the architects' and designers' offices and excludes any liability. The publisher assumes no responsibility for its accuracy or completeness as well as copyright discrepancies and refers to the specified sources (architects' and designers' offices). All rights to the photographs are property of the photographer (please refer to the picture).